T0361796

ROUTLEDGE LIBRARY EDITIONS:
DEVELOPMENT

PERSISTENT UNDERDEVELOPMENT

PERSISTENT UNDERDEVELOPMENT
Change and Economic Modernization in the West Indies

JAY R. MANDLE

Volume 47

Routledge
Taylor & Francis Group

LONDON AND NEW YORK

First published in 1996

This edition first published in 2011
by Routledge
2 Park Square, Milton Park, Abingdon, Oxon, OX14 4RN

Simultaneously published in the USA and Canada
by Routledge
270 Madison Avenue, New York, NY 10016

Routledge is an imprint of the Taylor & Francis Group, an informa business

© 1996 OPA (Overseas Publishers Association)

British Library Cataloguing in Publication Data
A catalogue record for this book is available from the British Library

ISBN 13: 978-0-415-58414-2 (Set)
eISBN 13: 978-0-203-84035-1 (Set)
ISBN 13: 978-0-415-59364-9 (Volume 47)
eISBN 13: 978-0-203-83842-6 (Volume 47)

Publisher's Note
The publisher has gone to great lengths to ensure the quality of this reprint but
points out that some imperfections in the original copies may be apparent.

Disclaimer
The publisher has made every effort to trace copyright holders and welcomes
correspondence from those they have been unable to contact.

Persistent Underdevelopment

Change and Economic Modernization in the West Indies

Jay R. Mandle

Colgate University
Hamilton, New York

Gordon and Breach Publishers

Australia China France Germany India Japan Luxembourg
Malaysia The Netherlands Russia Singapore Switzerland
Thailand United Kingdom United States

Emmaplein 5
1075 AW Amsterdam
The Netherlands

Cover: Photograph taken by Joan D. Mandle.

British Library Cataloguing in Publication Data

Mandle, Jay R.
  Persistent Underdevelopment: Change and
  Economic Modernization in the West
  Indies. – (Caribbean Studies,ISSN
  0275-5793;Vol.10)
  I. Title II. Series
  330.9729

  ISBN   2-88449-193-7   (hardcover)
         2-88449-194-5   (softcover)

CONTENTS

INTRODUCTION TO THE SERIES

The purpose of this series is to provide a forum in which the major themes and trends affecting the entire Caribbean region will be explored in depth. Thus, while the island-specific approach is not eschewed, the aim is to develop perspectives on problem-solving in the area as an entirety, both on the local level and in the international context. Hence the emphasis is on the qualitative and quantitative interpretation of the economic and political culture in which the modern Caribbean operates. Historical, demographical and sociological issues, when relevant to the central focus of the series, will also be examined.

Caribbean Studies publishes the research of academic scholars working within the region, as well as Caribbeanists working internationally. Simultaneously, it is hoped that the volumes function as a reference data source for libraries, foundations and government agencies with an interest in the Caribbean, either exclusively or peripherally.

It is the editors' hope that the series will increase comprehensive Caribbean studies internationally and will similarly stimulate innovative research and development of methodology suitable to comparative perspectives. Only when the Caribbean is evaluated in its broadest panorama can the true global importance of the region be appreciated.

PREFACE

This book began as a revision of my 1982 publication, *Patterns of Caribbean Development: An Interpretive Essay on Economic Change*. My interest in preparing such a revision was stimulated by a series of discussions with the publisher, who convinced me that a revisiting of the themes addressed in that book would be timely. *Patterns* had attempted to explain why the countries of the Caribbean were not economically developed and to root that explanation in the region's historical experience. In it, I offered a definition of development which was not so narrow that countries which merely were experiencing a rise in per capita output were considered developing. But at the same time, I wanted my definition of development not to be excessively broad. I wanted to avoid the temptation of considering as developed only those societies of whose political and social organization I approved. In that regard, *Patterns* offered an analytic framework rooted in the work of Karl Marx and Simon Kuznets. This approach continues to inform the current work.

The study of underdevelopment has suffered from a lack of empirical work, a shortfall which *Patterns* was intended to help reduce. At least until quite recently, it was commonly believed that underdevelopment was the result of the inevitable exploitation which poor countries experienced in their relationship with rich countries. In this framework, it was argued that participation in world markets acted to retard development and that the onset of development awaited a country's exit or decoupling from world markets. Recent growth, particularly in East Asia, has necessitated a fundamental rethinking of this conventional wisdom. But as yet, there are still only a few historically specific examinations of the absence of modernization in today's poor countries. Similarly, there is not yet a rich vein of work investigating the conditions which have to be satisfied for modernization to be experienced in countries which previously were thought to be underdeveloped. Thus, though doubt has been cast on a theory such as dependency — which hypothesizes the inevitability of exploitation and growth retardation when poor countries deal with rich ones — it remains the case that our understanding is still inadequate concerning the reasons why economic growth has spread only to a limited extent geographically.

Once I had initiated the revision, I quickly discovered that what I was doing was not a revision at all. Rather, I was writing an entirely new book. The passage of time had, in the first place, resulted in a substantial growth in the scholarly literature on Caribbean development and economic history. These new additions compelled a response on my part. In some cases they provided enrichment and expansion of my discussion; in others they necessitated a change in my views; and in yet others at least a dialogue was called for. In contrast to the experience of writing *Patterns*, where I felt handicapped by a lack of scholarly writing, in this case there was more than enough analysis to bolster my efforts.

Second, *Patterns* had been entirely neglectful of events which I now believe *could* and therefore *should* be analyzed. The experiences of the People's Revolutionary Government in Grenada between 1979 and 1983 was one such event. Writing in the early 1980s, I lacked both sufficient data and adequate historical perspective upon which to evaluate the policies of the government of Maurice Bishop. More than ten years after the tragic demise of the PRG, it is now possible to evaluate what was done in Grenada in these years. It is, however, *now* only possible to do so. Just as importantly, such an analysis of the PRG experience may help to inform other and new strategies of development. This will be important, particularly, if in the current period the strategies offered by the World Bank and International Monetary Fund prove to be inadequate, as I believe will be the case.

Similarly, *Patterns* contained no discussion of the economic development of either Barbados or the countries which belong to the Organization of Eastern Caribbean States — Antigua and Barbuda, Dominica, St. Kitts and Nevis, St. Lucia, and St. Vincent and the Grenadines, as well as Grenada. The increased availability of data and the growth of a scholarly literature particularly concerning Barbados has allowed me to provide analyses of these countries, thereby overcoming an important shortfall present in the earlier volume. Thus, in this book there is extensive coverage of issues which were totally absent from the previous work.

I have also been able to extend the discussion of the experiences of Trinidad and Tobago, Jamaica and Guyana — countries explored in *Patterns*. Particularly, the aftermath of the petroleum boom in Trinidad and Tobago deserved extensive treatment. If ever it needed to be established that the availability of financing is at best the necessary but not the sufficient condition for the onset of modern economic growth, a study of Trinidad and Tobago does so. The boom of the 1970s and the collapse of the 1980s stands as powerful support for the view that more is required in development than the capacity to purchase plants and equipment.

Patterns included a chapter on Cuba. In it I discussed that country's ambivalent attitude towards the development of a private sector in the economy. I was encouraged by what I took to be "recent evidence suggesting that the Cuban leadership has begun to rethink its perverse policies with regard to the private sector" (p. 89). As things turned out, that optimism proved to be unwarranted. Cuba throughout the 1980s failed to encourage the private sector development which I believed, and *still* believe, integral to that country's economic modernization. In the meantime, however, the collapse of communism has thrown Cuba into crisis. Sources of supply for both materials and credit have dried up as have markets for Cuba's output, worsening the already difficult prospects that country faces in attempting to achieve development. In the current effort I concluded that it would be best to drop the discussion of Cuba altogether, for reasons not dissimilar to those which led me to exclude Grenada from the earlier work. It is too early even to speculate about the direction Cuba will take to extricate itself from its current difficulties, and obviously far too soon to make any meaningful statements concerning the likelihood of success in this regard.

This book finally, much more than the earlier one, deals with the migration of the Caribbean people and the role of education in West Indies development. In addition, the heightened presence of the World Bank and the International Monetary Fund in the region requires analysis. The fact that all of the four larger territories in the region — Barbados, Guyana, Jamaica, and Trinidad and Tobago — have accepted conditions insisted upon by these multilateral institutions in exchange for balance of payments support is an important new ingredient in economic policy making not previously present in the West Indies.

Although much has changed in the region since I wrote *Patterns*, the conclusions which are reached in this book, like those in the earlier study, are not optimistic. In the earlier volume I concluded that Guyana, Jamaica, and Trinidad and Tobago had all failed to discover the means by which to achieve modern economic growth. Whatever optimism was present was reserved for Cuba, an optimism which, as noted above, proved to be erroneous.

In the current work, I am still unable to come to optimistic conclusions concerning the future of modern economic growth in the Commonwealth Caribbean. Such economic expansion as has occurred in recent years has been confined to the smaller islands, especially those which have benefitted from the expansion of the tourist industry and increased revenues generated by the export of bananas. But these industries do not provide the region with the technological capacity which is key to economic development. As a result, though growth has occurred, development remains an unlikely outcome. Elsewhere, in the larger territories, economic decline rather than growth has been the more typical experience. Perhaps there is a cause for optimism in Guyana simply based on the demise of the Burnham regime. But it is far too early to determine whether the programs adopted by the People's Progressive Party/Civic Government, in an uneasy alliance with the World Bank and the International Monetary Fund, will launch the long delayed onset of growth in that country. Elsewhere, neither Jamaica nor Trinidad and Tobago has provided much evidence in the recent historic record to conclude that the path to modernization has been embarked upon.

This book is the result of many years of observing, living in, and thinking about economic development and the Caribbean. It is not easy or pleasant on the basis of such a commitment to conclude that the region, for which my family and I possess a huge stock of affection, has failed to solve the central problems of economic modernization. It is of course true that many Caribbean people, as individuals, have solved that problem. All too frequently, however, these successes in modern economic life have involved emigration and settlement outside of the Caribbean, most frequently in the United States. In such cases, the Caribbean itself only marginally benefits from these successful adaptations. The fact remains that the trajectory currently experienced in the region provides, at the moment, little basis for any other conclusion than that the West Indies in the foreseeable future will not set out on the path of successful modern economic growth.

Especially in a work which has extended over as many years as this one, it is impossible to thank everyone who has contributed and helped shape my thinking. I do wish to acknowledge the suggestions for revision and rethinking which I received from Lou Ferleger, Stan Engerman, Isadore Reivich, Jon Mandle and Joan Mandle. They of course are not to be held responsible for errors which remain in my analysis.

CHAPTER 1

The Content of Economic Development

The study of economic development in the Caribbean has been hampered by the fact that no consensus prevails in the region concerning the definition of that process. Disagreement on the content of development means that discussions of the subject often are exercises in frustration. In the absence of a common understanding of the meaning of economic development fruitful dialogue is impossible. Further, this absence has meant that policy has been undertaken largely in a theoretical vacuum. Without a solid academic consensus over the objectives of development policy, politicians have been left without clear guidelines concerning the targets towards which their policies should be aimed.

Illustrative of the problem are recent papers by two of the region's most distinguished economists. Norman Girvan in a paper entitled "Rethinking Development: Out Loud" reviews the failure of dependency theory, and considers as an alternative paradigm the concepts of "sustained development" and "Human Scale Development." What seems to attract Girvan in these approaches is their attempt "to integrate the nonmaterial with the material in a schema that better captures the totality of human existence." After having concluded his discussion, he, however, asks, "so where does all this leave us?" and answers, "frankly, I am not too sure myself: If you [the reader] find that there have been more questions than answers in what I have said, then you are right."[1]

In contrast, the Guyanese economist, C.Y. Thomas has no such doubts. He lists eight elements in indicating "what development (as the negation of under-development) means in the Caribbean context." Development for

1

Thomas 1) "requires a system of ownership, control and production oriented towards satisfying the basic needs of the masses"; 2) necessitates "implementation of the right to work"; it should be 3) self-reliant 4) democratic; 5) preserve the environment; 6) needs a democratic state which would have an important role to play in the process; though 7) it will have to be sensitive to the geopolitical domination of the United States in the process and 8) be part of a regional process of transformation.[2]

Though in many ways the objectives enumerated by Thomas are attractive, they by no means can stand as the criteria by which to measure the presence or absence of economic development. The first of his standards concerning the institutional configuration of the economy and the basic needs of the population is insufficiently specified. Merely referring to the structure of ownership and management does not necessarily yield agreement concerning the set of property rights which would result in both equality and growth. Similarly, it is not at all clear what Thomas means when he refers to the "basic needs of the masses." If this is meant to indicate the providing of the necessities adequate to sustain life then to a large extent even the economies of the Caribbean have satisfied that goal. In all likelihood, however, Thomas has a more expansive definition of needs in mind, a definition which must be made explicit to make his goal operational.

Thomas' other criteria are far too broad and demanding. Their strict application would in all likelihood lead to the conclusion that no country on the earth has ever been economically developed. Even a country such as the United States would fail his test of development since it has not been able to sustain full employment for its labor force and has not done at all well on environmental issues. At the same time the countries of the former socialist bloc, though perhaps satisfying the basic needs of their populations and achieving full employment, certainly could not be considered democratic.

Acceptance of Thomas' definition would leave unanswered the question of what accounts for differences in living standards among countries. It is that set of differences in material well-being which underscores the gap between developed and underdeveloped countries. Thomas seems to want to reserve the phrase economic development for democratic and egalitarian societies. The fact is, however, historical experience suggests that broad increases in consumption and production can and do occur in a variety of social and political settings, certainly not only in those specified by Thomas. Thomas, in short, offers us not a definition of economic development, but rather his view of the good society. What is required is not that, but an approach which provides insight into how and why some countries have been able better to satisfy the material needs of their citizens than others. It could plausibly be argued that the advances in the standard of living associated with modern economic growth represent the necessary but not sufficient condition for the construction of a good society. But this is not what Thomas argues, leaving his discussion as an inadequate base from which to examine the Caribbean's development problems.

A more useful approach to this question has been provided by the late Simon Kuznets. Kuznets won the Nobel Prize in economics on the basis of his cross national empirical study of the growth experience. According to Richard A. Easterlin it was he "more than any other individual [who] has identified and analyzed 'modern economic growth.'"[3] Thus, what we are dealing with in the definition of modern growth offered by Kuznets is not an abstract model. Rather it is one which is rooted in the historical experience of the countries which were successful in sustaining advances in levels of per capita output and becoming economically developed.

According to Kuznets,

> The basic feature of modern economic growth, as it has been observed in the more developed countries since the late 18th century, is that the rise in per capita or per worker product was associated largely with extended application of a growing stock of useful knowledge, via technological innovations in production.

In turn, the high rate of growth of per capita product which results from that technological innovation in production

> required and was accompanied by, rapid shifts in production and social structure — usually referred to as industrialization, urbanization, movement of labor force to employee status, and the like.[4]

Kuznets' findings and his characterization of the process of economic modernization are generally supportive of the way Marx more than a century ago understood capitalist expansion. G.A. Cohen writes that for Marx:

> the development of scientific knowledge is ... the centre of the development of the productive forces. In its higher stages the development of the productive forces ... merges with the development of productively useful science.[5]

As Marx himself put it, "the growth of the productive forces of labour means merely that less direct labour is required in order to make a larger product."[6] Thus it is safe to assume that when Marx refers to an advance in the forces of production he is referring to the same phenomenon Kuznets describes as modern economic growth.

For both Marx and Kuznets, technological change is the proximate source of economic development, but its rate of advance is itself the consequence of the institutional configuration and ideology dominant in the country in question. Formulated analytically, both believe that technological change can be seen as the dependent variable whose level and rate of growth are influenced by independent variables, broadly understood to be institutions and ideologies. Thus, Kuznets is explicit in arguing that "if advancing technology is to be employed efficiently and widely, and, indeed, if its own progress is to be stimulated by such use, institutional and ideological adjustments must be made to effect the proper use of innovations generated by the advancing stock of human knowledge."[7]

Writing in the nineteenth century, when the first fruits of the development experience were becoming obvious, Marx was optimistic that the growth process would spread internationally. By contrast, Kuznets in the twentieth century, knew that it had not. Thus, Marx believed that "the country that is more developed industrially only shows to the less developed the image of its own future." Growth would be experienced universally because capitalism, "compels all nations, on pain of extinction, to adopt the bourgeois mode of production; it compels them to introduce what it calls civilization into their midst, i.e., to become bourgeois themselves. In a word it creates a world after its own image."[8] Kuznets, on the other hand, writing in the early 1980s believed that underdevelopment is "likely to remain with us for the very long future."[9]

Marx believed that it was capitalism's organization which promoted economic growth. Alan Richards in his discussion of development in Marxian economics argues that "For Marx, the rapid discovery and diffusion of technological innovations under capitalism was a consequence of the distribution of access to land, labor power and produced means of production: only when these were governed by capitalist rules of the game did people search so hungrily for new knowledge and for new techniques of producing commodities."[10] For Marx it was the growth of "civil society" which was decisive both to the emergence of capitalism and development. According to Avineri, Marx believed that

> what ultimately gave rise to the bourgeois world and industrialization was the slow differentiation of a sphere of activity which legitimized profit-oriented economic activity as an autonomous field, no more encumbered by the ethical, religious, and political restriction of the feudal order.[11]

Capitalism's culture, unlike prior historical epochs, allows for the unrestricted introduction of new methods of production. It also authenticates economic competition and labor mobility thereby accelerating productivity growth and the emergence of new industries. In combination these result in a technological dynamism never present before in human history. Marx writes in the *Grundrisse* that "development of the productive forces of social labour is the historical task and justification of capital." This view was even more clearly expressed in *The Communist Manifesto* where Marx and Engels write that the "constant revolutionizing of production, uninterrupted disturbance of all social conditions, everlasting uncertainty and agitation distinguish the bourgeois epoch from all earlier ones."[12]

Marx is consistent in this view even where capitalism is introduced through colonialism. In an article entitled "The Future Results of British Rule in India," published in 1853, Marx argues that with British investment in railroads, economic development in the subcontinent will be triggered. He writes:

> when you have once introduced machinery into the locomotion of a country which possesses iron and coal, you are unable to withhold it from its fabrication.... The railway system will therefore become, in India, the forerunner of modern industry.

England, according to Marx:

> has to fulfill a double mission in India: one destructive, the other regenerating — the annihilation of the old Asiatic society and the laying of material foundations of Western society in Asia.[13]

Marx anticipated, as Kiernan has emphasized, that colonialism would not only lead to the industrialization of India by the British, "but he was hopeful of something even better, industrialization by Indian enterprise."[14]

Marx clearly was overly sanguine concerning the spread of economic growth. Data on 19th century growth is spotty at best. But the most widely accepted estimates of the growth in Gross Domestic Product per capita, prepared by Angus Maddison and reproduced in Table 1, provide at least an idea of the delay in the onset of development in what was to become the Third World. Growth in the Third World by and large was negligible in each of the three periods estimated by Maddison between 1820 and 1950, in no period exceeding 1 percent per year. By contrast when, after 1950, modern growth did spread rapidly, growth rates were greater than 2.5 percent annually.

Most Marxists reacted to this limited spread of economic development by reversing the position held by Marx himself. Instead, they argued that the spread of capitalism from Europe and North American to less developed areas no longer was necessarily associated with modern economic growth. Marx's optimistic view of the impact of Great Britain in India was abandoned. Thus in 1928 at the Sixth Congress of the Communist International in a discussion of revolutionary movements in colonial and semi-colonial countries a distinction was drawn between

> those colonies which have served the capitalist countries as colonizing regions for their surplus population and which in this way have become exten-

Table 1

Growth of GDP per Capita
(annual average compound growth rates)

Country	1820–70	1870–1913	1913–50	1950–73	1973–80
Argentina		1.5	0.6	2.2	0.1
Bangladesh				0.7	2.5
Brazil	0.1	1.2	1.6	4.3	5.0
China	0.0	0.5	–0.4	4.0	3.7
Colombia			1.3	2.3	3.1
Egypt			0.2	1.7	6.6
Ghana		0.9	1.1	1.2	–3.0
India	0.0	0.6	–0.1	1.4	1.7
Mexico	0.0	0.8	1.7	3.1	2.4
Pakistan				1.7	2.2
Peru			2.2	2.7	–0.7
Philippines			–0.3	2.9	3.6
South Korea			–0.9	4.7	4.9
Spain			–0.3	5.9	1.0
Thailand				4.0	4.4
Turkey				3.2	2.3
Arithmetic mean	0.0	0.9	0.6	2.8	2.5

Source: Angus Maddison, "A Comparison of Levels of GDP Per Capita in Developed and Developing Countries, 1700–1980," *The Journal of Economic History*, Vol. XLIII, No. 1 (March 1983), Table 1, p. 28.

sions of the capitalist system (Australia, Canada etc.), and those which are exploited by the imperialist primarily as markets for their commodities, as sources of raw materials and as spheres for capital investment.

Colonies which have absorbed surplus population became "members of the given imperialist system with equal or nearly equal rights." But in colonies of the second type "the ruling imperialism is related to the colonial countries primarily as a parasite, sucking the blood from the economic organism." To be sure, in this situation there is

> some encouragement of colonial production [but] this is directed on such lines and promoted only in such a degree as corresponded to the interests of the metropolis and in particular to the interests of the preservation of its colonial monopoly.

As a result,

> colonial forms of capitalist exploitation ... hinder the development of the productive forces of the colony.... Real industrialization of the colonial country, in particular the building up of a flourishing engineering industry which would promote the independent development of the productive forces, is not encouraged but on the contrary is hindered by the metropolis.[15]

Thus a revision of Marx had been issued. Colonialism did not always represent the spread of capitalism. A colonialism of exploitation was hypothesized; one which would constrain, not stimulate, development.

This negative hypothesis concerning capitalism's ability to foster development in the Third World gained wide acceptance among Marxists. Especially during the 1950s and 1960s, when extensive attention was directed to the problems of underdeveloped countries, Marxist opinion was virtually unanimous in agreeing that integration in the world capitalist economy ensured the continued underdevelopment of the poor countries of Asia, Africa and Latin America. Probably the most sophisticated expression of this view was contained in Paul A. Baran's 1957 publication, *The Political Economy of Growth.*

In this book Baran compares the unsuccessful development experience of India and contrasts that to the process of growth which occurred in Japan, "the only Asian country that succeeded in escaping its neighbors' fate ... in attaining a relatively high degree of economic advancement." The contrast between the two, according to Baran, is traceable to the fact that India suffered from British colonialism and Japan escaped such domination. The British in India retarded development not only because of the drain of resources which occurred under colonialism. Indian development was also harmed because colonialism destroyed "the entire framework of Indian society." As such, British policy "broke down whatever beginnings there were of an indigenous industrial development." By contrast, Japan was not disrupted. Capital accumulation occurred before the Meiji Revolution and the latter in turn, created "the political and economic framework indispensable for capitalist development." Of particular importance in this regard was "the dominant part played by the government in accelerating the development of industrial capitalism." All of this occurred, according to Baran because "Japan is the only country in Asia (and in Africa and in Latin America) that escaped being turned into a colony or dependency of Western European or American capitalism, that had a chance of independent national development."[16] Thus it is that Baran provided Marxists with a theory which reversed Marx's optimistic assessment about the international spread of capitalist development.

Building on Baran's work, many Marxists and those influenced by Marxism elaborated a theory which explained how it was that modern capitalism was not capable of stimulating the process of modernization in the Third World. In general the argument was that imperialism prevented an indigenous growth-promoting capitalism from appearing in today's poor nations. Rather, the growth of their economies was stunted by their insertion in the world economy in a permanently subordinate role. In their integration in world markets the poor countries were made to be dependent upon and exploited by the wealthier states. In this relationship a transfer of wealth occurred from the poor to the rich. That in turn, prevented the Third World countries from progressing, while contributing to the continued expansion of the rich. Not all Marxists adopted this approach. In particular Bill Warren in 1973 published a self-consciously iconoclastic article defending Marx's original view concerning capitalism's growth-generating characteristics.[17] Despite this dissent however the dominant view among Marxists during the 1960s and 1970s was that capitalism was incapable of achieving economic growth in underdeveloped countries.

It is not surprising that writing a hundred years later than Marx and having observed the emergence of a gap between countries experiencing the development process and those which did not, Kuznets adopts a more historically accurate view of the spread of development than did Marx. The limits to the spread of development were too obvious to ignore. But Kuznets, in contrast to twentieth century Marxists, believed that growth in the contemporary period remained a realistic possibility. Indeed he wrote that given the availability of modern technology, "all LDCs may be considered *developable*." He goes on, however, to insist that it does not follow from this potential that success will necessarily result. Failure is possible because "the LDCs are characterized by major social and institutional constraints that make it impossible for them to exploit the technological potential adequately." It would not, Kuznets writes, "be difficult to list a range of social and institutional weaknesses in LDCs that can be blamed for their inability to use much of the current long-term technological potential, and their continuing to use ... the older and less productive techniques." He concludes:

> Patterns of behavior, social institutions, priorities of values — all surviving from the premodern past, are translated into a system of organization of land

ownership and tenure that inhibit productive agriculture; into scarcity of skilled labor and of entrepreneurship that make it impossible to adopt modern nonagricultural technology. Weakness of existing material and human infrastructure, and instability and weakness of the political system, unable to count on effective consensus relating to values that would encourage economic modernization, deserve a special note.[18]

For Kuznets, then, underdevelopment is caused by institutions and/or ideologies which constrain the adoption of modern technology. In this context he identifies "two major groups of factors [which] ... limited the spread of modern economic growth." The first is the absence of a political and social framework "capable of accommodating rapid structural change and resolving the conflicts that it generates, while encouraging the growth-promoting groups in society." The second is the external policies of developed countries. Kuznets writes that "the increasingly national cast of organization in developed countries made for policies toward other parts of the world that, while introducing some modern economic and social elements, were, in many areas, clearly inhibiting." Such policies Kuznets writes "ranged from the imposition of colonial status to other limitations on political freedom." The result of these policies was that even in the contemporary period, "Political independence and removal of the inferior status of the native members of the community, rather than economic advance were given top priority."[19]

But while Kuznets points to both internal and external constraints to development, the fact is that growth in poor nations did accelerate rapidly after World War II. As indicated in Table 1, the growth experienced in the poor countries, after 1950 was substantially higher than had ever before occurred. In the Kuznets framework, such an acceleration of growth could only have meant that "favorable changes must have occurred in the LDCs capacity to reduce social and institutional obstacles to the use of modern technology; and or major improvements in the international framework of trade and other ties within which the given LDCs could operate." Indeed, Kuznets believed that "only radical shifts can account for a sharp break toward much higher growth rates sustained over a substantial time span."[20]

Kuznets illustrates what he had in mind in a brief examination of the acceleration in economic growth which occurred in Taiwan in the years after 1945. There he found the "radical break" which he believed was necessary to stimulate growth in poor countries. The first element was Taiwan's achieving of sovereignty. After "five decades under colonial occupation by Japan and for half a decade as a necessarily neglected province of greater China," sovereignty provided "both unity and the basis of a long series of internal policy decisions," allowing it to "take advantage of favorable trade and other external ties." Political independence provided Taiwan with the possibility of tapping into the existing stock of technological knowledge and accelerating its growth.[21]

But sovereignty according to Kuznets was only a necessary, not a sufficient condition for the launching of Taiwanese modernization. The assumption of political responsibility did not mean that Taiwan would necessarily avoid "errors in choosing among policy alternatives." Internal factors were responsible for that. Among the reasons that Taiwanese policy was successful in avoiding mistakes was "the human skills of the largely agricultural Island population," the island leadership's experience in policy making and "detachment from Taiwan's past institutions and established group interests." External relations, particularly the assistance of the United States and economic ties with Japan were also important in the island's acceleration of growth. A variety of circumstances, in short, conspired to provide this "small, less developed market economy in which the main comparative advantage lay in human capital (not in natural resources), with [an] orientation to rapidly increasing participation in international trade and international division of labor."[22] This participation, in turn, produced a breakthrough in the economic modernization process.

Kuznets' comments with regard to Taiwan are obviously relevant to the case at hand. The Caribbean too can be seen as a region in which only to a limited extent do natural resources provide a comparative advantage. Bauxite in Jamaica and Guyana and petroleum in Trinidad and Tobago do offer opportunities in the aluminum and energy industries. Elsewhere the region's salubrious climate, sand and sea provide the natural endowments which are supportive of a tourist industry. In general, however, for the region to prosper a wider economic foundation is required than is represented by these assets. The people of the Caribbean, like the Taiwanese, are required to use their ingenuity and technical skills to advance economically. Following in the Kuznets' tradition, then, this study will attempt to identify the circumstances which have in the past and continue in the present to constrain the ability of the people of the Caribbean to be successful innovators in the international economy.

GROWTH AND HUMAN DEVELOPMENT

Even if neo-Marxism is wrong in hypothesizing the impossibility of capitalist economic modernization, a larger issue still remains unanswered. That question is the extent to which the development experience results in an advance in the well-being of typical members of the population. In this regard there is an extensive literature, again extending back to Marx, which adopts a pessimistic view on this subject. It acknowledges that economic development may occur, but maintains that this process means little positive for the well-being of most people.

Marx and Engels were the pioneers in hypothesizing the simultaneous process of economic advance and immizeration. In the *Communist Manifesto* they wrote that "the bourgeoisie, during its rule of scarce one hundred years, has created more massive and modern colossal productive forces than all preceding generations together." At the same time, however, "in this process the modern labourer ... instead of rising, sinks deeper and deeper below the conditions of existence of his own class."[23] Twenty years later, in *Capital*, Marx offered a more nuanced view which still remained essentially pessimistic:

> The greater the social wealth, the functioning capital, the extent and energy of its growth, and therefore, also, the absolute mass of the proletariat and the productiveness of its labour, the greater is the industrial reserve army [of the unemployed]. The same causes which develop the expansive power of capital, developes (sic) also the labour-power at its disposal. The relative mass of the industrial reserve-army increases therefore with the potential energy of wealth. But the greater this reserve-army in proportion to the active labour-army, the greater is the mass of a consolidated surplus-population, whose misery is in inverse ratio to its torment of labour. The more extensive, finally, the lazarus-layers of the working-class, the greater is official pauperism.[24]

Whether Marx was right in his pessimism concerning the effects of European industrialization and development is still being debated. Adelman and Morris at least in a 1978 article appear to come down on the pessimistic side, arguing that "the early stage of economic progress in the first part of the 19th century was usually characterized by unfavorable impacts on the very poor." In contrast, Jeffrey G. Williamson, though conceding that early industrialization did result in rising income inequality, nonetheless denies that most such countries experienced an increase in poverty rates.[25] If it were established that the pessimists were right and that economic modernization typically results in a decline in the living standards of the poor, the growth process would be faced with a serious indictment. But to date no such consensus exists.

The focus of this debate, however, is too narrow to allow for a full consideration of the social impact of economic modernization. In all three of the cases cited above — Marx, Adelman and Morris, and Williamson — the discussion centers on the extent of the deprivation modernization visits on those at the bottom of society. But a broad consideration of the effects of economic growth necessitates dealing with the modal experience as well as those at the extremes. It is essential to identify what happens to the quality of life for most of the people, not simply those who are the least successful participants in the process. By focusing on the poor as the most important issue, the extent to which the growth process has wide direct and personal implications is begged. Though of great importance, the fate of the poorest in society provides a distorted picture if it is the single issue addressed.

Insight into the general impact of economic growth on welfare can be provided by employing the Human Development Index (HDI), a measure developed by the United Nations Development Program (UNDP). In producing this index, the UNDP argues that it is superior to "previous concepts of development [which] have often given exclusive attention to economic growth — on the assumption that growth will ultimately benefit everyone." That is, the HDI was constructed because of doubts that growth necessarily provides universal benefits. Its purpose precisely is to determine the extent to which growth does advance human welfare generally.[26] Underlying the HDI is the view that human development is a "process of enlarging people's choices" and that "the objective of development is that people can enjoy long, healthy and creative lives."[27]

To operationalize that concept the UNDP constructs an index which includes three components: longevity, knowledge, and a measure which taps income distribution. Countries are ranked relative to each other in these areas. Longevity is measured by life expectancy at birth and knowledge is measured by adult literacy and mean years of schooling. The income variable assumes that diminishing returns to income prevails and becomes greater to the extent that income exceeds the poverty level. Thus countries with relatively few people at or below the poverty level score higher on this measure than those where there is a high proportion of individuals receiving incomes that result in poverty.[28] Though the HDI was constructed to rank countries for a particular period of time it can also be constructed to measure changes over time. Looking at changes in the measure will suggest which countries were most successful in advancing human well-being. With that done, it is then possible to determine what if any relationship exists between such progress and the more narrowly defined process of modern economic growth. In this way the extent to which growth really is associated with advances in welfare can be determined. Conventionally measured economic growth may only be loosely or perhaps not at all associated with improvement in people's well-being. If so then the pessimists' hypothesis concerning the impact of development on welfare would receive support. On the other hand if there is a close relationship between measures of economic growth and advances in the HDI then the optimistic case would find support.

To examine this relationship we collected data on changes in HDI between 1970 and 1990 for seventy-two countries, none of which did the UNDP consider economically developed. We then collected data on economic growth for these same countries during roughly the same years.[29] The linear regression analysis which then was carried out on these two data sets resulted in support for the hypothesis that economic growth produces enhanced human welfare. There is a statistically significant positive relationship between growth in GNP per capita and changes in the HDI index. For this grouping of seventy-two countries the coefficient of determination (r^2) was 0.4599. This statistic indicates that close to half of the variation in the HDI index can be accounted for by differences in the economic growth rate. Taken as a whole this analysis strongly supports the view that economic modernization has a positive impact on the well-being of the population in countries experiencing that process.

A closer examination of these data reinforces support for the hypothesis that economic growth raises the level of human welfare. Tables 2 and 3 provide information on the ten best and the ten worst HDI performers. Among the ten countries with the largest advances in HDI the economic growth rate was a robust 4.0 percent per year. Among the ten countries in which the HDI experience was worst, economic decline was experienced in six nations, resulting in a –0.8 growth rate percent per year for all ten. This difference in the economic growth experience of those nations successful in raising their HDI and those which were not represents additional support for the optimistic view.

A possible flaw in this comparison lies in the fact that the countries in which the HDI grew the most tended to be more economically advanced than the countries which saw the least increase in HDI. The average ranking in GNP per capita of the countries with the largest increase in HDI was 53rd in the world compared to 88th for the poor performers. To investigate the importance of the level of development on the association between growth and HDI performance, Table 4 collects data on countries at roughly the same level of economic development as those grouped in Table 2. The countries in Table 4, however, were selected because they did poorly in their HDI experience between 1970 and 1990. Thus we are able to hold the level of economic development constant while comparing a grouping of countries which were successful in their HDI experience (Table 2) with those which were not (Table 4). What we are looking for here is whether while holding the level of economic development constant in this way, we continue to find that those nations which did well in the HDI index experienced more substantial economic growth than was the case among countries which did not see their HDI index rise.

Table 2

Change in Human Development Index, 1970–90, Average Annual Rate of Growth of Gross National Product Per Capita, 1965–90 and Ranking of Countries by Gross National Product per Capita, 1990 for Countries with Largest Increase in HDI

Countries	Change in HDI	Average annual change in GNP per capita	GNP per capita ranking
Korea	0.282	7.1	29
Mauritius	0.268	3.2	51
Malaysia	0.251	4.0	50
Tunisia	0.247	3.2	62
Syria	0.233	2.9	70
Botswana	0.215	8.4	54
Indonesia	0.176	4.5	90
Gabon	0.175	0.9	32
Algeria	0.175	2.1	53
Brazil	0.170	3.3	36
Mean	0.219	4.0	53

Source: United Nations Development Programme, *Human Development Report 1992* (New York: Oxford University Press, 1992), Technical Note Table 1.3, p. 94; World Bank, *World Development Report, 1992* (New York: Oxford University Press, 1992), Table 1, p. 218–219.

As a comparison of Tables 2 and 4 indicates, even when the level of development is held constant, the same pattern appears. The countries in which the HDI grew slowly experienced a mean economic growth rate of only 0.3 percent per year, compared to 4.0 percent among the nations most successful in raising their HDI. Both sets of comparisons then point to the conclusion that economic growth promotes advances in HDI.

Table 3

Change in Human Development Index, 1970–90, Average Annual Rate of Growth of Gross National Product per Capita, 1965–90 and Ranking of Countries by Gross National Product per Capita, 1990 for Countries with Least Increase in HDI

Countries	Change in HDI	Average annual change in GNP per capita	GNP per capita ranking
Jamaica	–0.076	–1.3	61
Nicaragua	–0.053	–3.3	42
Uganda	–0.049	–2.4	112
Papua New Guinea	–0.022	0.1	75
Zambia	–0.006	–1.9	95
Benin	–0.006	–0.1	103
Burkina Faso	0.001	1.3	105
Rwanda	0.002	1.0	106
Sierra Leone	0.002	0.0	110
Peru	0.004	–0.2	66
Mean	–0.020	–0.8	88

Source: See Table 2.

The conclusion which follows therefore is that the process of modern economic growth not only possesses unique characteristics, centering on the application of productivity raising technology to production. It also tends to have beneficial effects on the well-being of the population concerned. To be sure not everyone is better off as a result of the process. But the fact is that it in general does promote a population's well-being.

Table 4

Change in Human Development Index, 1970–90, Average Annual Rate of Growth of Gross National product per Capita, 1965–90, and Ranking of Countries by Gross National Product per Capita, 1990 for Selected Countries

Countries	Change in HDI	Average annual change in GNP per capita	GNP per capita ranking
Jamaica	−0.076	−1.3	61
Nicaragua	−0.053	−3.3	42
Peru	0.004	−0.2	66
El Salvador	0.015	−0.4	68
Panama	0.028	1.4	57
Paraguay	0.031	4.6	67
Argentina	0.049	−0.3	49
Uruguay	0.081	0.8	37
Iran	0.083	0.1	48
Mean	0.015	0.3	57

Source: See Table 2.

NOTES

1. Norman P. Girvan, "Rethinking Development: Out Loud," in Judith Wedderburn (ed.), *Rethinking Development* (Kingston, Jamaica: Consortium Graduate School of Social Sciences, 1991), p. 12.

2. C.Y. Thomas, "Alternative Development Models for the Caribbean," in Stanley Lalta and Marie Freckleton (eds.), *Caribbean Economic Development: The First Generation* (Kingston, Jamaica: Ian Randle Publishers, 1993), pp. 317–323.

3. Richard A. Easterlin, "Foreword," in Simon Kuznets, *Economic Development, the Family and Income Distribution: Selected Essays* (New York: Cambridge University Press, 1989), p. 1.

4. Simon Kuznets, "Modern Economic Growth and the Less Developed Countries," in Simon Kuznets, *Economic Development, the Family, and Income Distribution*, pp. 68–69.

5. G.A. Cohen, *Karl Marx's Theory of History: A Defense* (Princeton: Princeton University Press, 1978), p. 45.

6. Marx, *Grundrisse*, p. 831, as cited in G.A. Cohen, *Karl Marx's Theory of History*, p. 55.

7. Simon Kuznets, "Modern Economic Growth: Findings and Reflections," in Simon Kuznets, *Population, Capital and Growth* (New York: W.W. Norton & Co. Inc., 1973), pp. 165–166.

8. Marx and Engels, "Manifesto of the Communist Party," as reprinted in Robert Freedman (ed.), *Marx on Economics* (New York: Harcourt, Brace & Co., 1961), p. 17; Karl Marx, *Capital: A Critique of Political Economy* (New York: The Modern Library, 1906), p. 13.

9. Simon Kuznets, "Modern Economic Growth and Less Developed Countries," p. 73.

10. Alan Richards, *Development and Modes of Production in Marxian Economics: A Critical Evaluation* (New York: Harwood Academic Publishers, 1986), p. 13.

11. Shlomo Avineri, "Marx and Modernization," *Review of Politics*, 31:2 (April 1969), p. 178.

12. Marx, *Grundrisse*, as quoted in G.A. Cohen, *Karl Marx's Theory of History*, p. 201, and Marx and Engels, "Manifesto of the Communist Party," as reprinted in Robert Freedman, ed., *Marx on Economics*, p. 15.

13. Quoted in Shlomo Avineri, "Marx and Modernization," pp. 132–133.

14. Victor Kiernan, "Marx and India," in Ralph Miliband and John Saville (eds.), *The Socialist Register, 1967* (New York: Monthly Review Press, 1967), p. 168.

15. "Extracts from the Theses on the Revolutionary Movement in Colonial and Semi-Colonial Countries adopted by the Sixth Comintern Congress," in Jane Degras (ed.), *The Communist International 1919–1943 Documents, II, 1923–1928* (London, New York, Toronto: Oxford University Press, 1960), p. 534.

16. Paul A. Baran, *The Political Economy of Growth* (New York: Monthly Review, Inc., 1957), pp. 151, 148, 149, 154, 157, 158.

17. Bill Warren, "Imperialism and Capitalist Industrialization," *New Left Review*, 81, September/October 1973; see also Patrick Clawson, "The Internationalization of Capital Accumulation," *The Insurgent Sociologist*, Spring 1977; Ian Roxborough, "Dependency Theory in the Sociology of Development: Some

Theoretical Problems," *Western African Journal of Sociology and Political Science*, Vol. 1, no. 2 (January 1976).

18. Simon Kuznets, "Modern Economic Growth and the Less Developed Countries," pp. 71–72.

19. Simon Kuznets, "Findings and Reflections," pp. 176–177.

20. Simon Kuznets, "Modern Economic Growth and Less Developed Countries," p. 73.

21. Simon Kuznets, "Modern Economic Growth and Less Developed Countries," pp. 73–74, 74–76.

22. Simon Kuznets, "Modern Economic Growth and Less Developed Countries," pp. 74, 75, 76.

23. Marx and Engels, "Manifesto of the Communist Party," as reprinted in Robert Freedman, *Marx on Economics*, pp. 17, 26.

24. Karl Marx, *Capital*, p. 707.

25. Irma Adelman and Cynthia Taft Morris, "Growth and Impoverishment in the Middle of the Nineteenth Century," *World Development*, 6:3, p. 246–247; Jeffrey G. Williamson, *Inequality, Poverty and History* (Cambridge, Mass: Basil Blackwell Inc., 1991), p. 137.

26. United Nations Development Programme, *Human Development Report 1992* (New York: Oxford University Press, 1992), p. 12.

27. Ibid., p. 12.

28. Ibid., pp. 91–97.

29. Data on the changes in HDI between 1970 and 1990 are taken from United Nations Development Programme, *Human Development Report 1992* (New York: Oxford University Press, 1992), Technical Note Table 1.3, p. 94. Information on changes in GNP per capita between 1965 and 1990 are taken from the World Bank, *World Development Report, 1992* (New York: Oxford University Press, 1992), Table 1, pp. 218–219.

CHAPTER 2

The Planation Economy and Economic Development

The Caribbean intellectual, Lloyd Best, writes that West Indian poverty is not caused by the weakness and fragility of the region's social institutions. Indeed, he emphasizes the deep-rooted nature and stability of those institutions, arguing that it is actually that strength which perpetuates underdevelopment. Best writes, "I can't see any way in which the Caribbean countries that I know are less developed than the more developed countries. What I see is that they're highly developed for poverty, which is something else. But the institutions are as deeply implanted, are highly developed mechanisms for doing whatever they are doing." The task of analysis, observes Best, is to explain how those institutions are "holding up the process of economic transformation."[1]

Because of its historical dominance in production, the West Indian sugar plantation must be the starting point in any examination of the institutions which contributed to the region's underdevelopment. The Caribbean is part of what Charles Wagley describes as Plantation America, a "culture sphere [which] extends spatially from about midway up the coast of Brazil into the Guianas, along the Caribbean coast, throughout the Caribbean itself and into the United States." Wagley writes that "sugar production by the plantation system with African slave labour became the fundamental formative feature of the Plantation-American culture sphere — and other crops such as cacao, coffee and later cotton were grown by a similar system."[2]

All of the societies of Plantation America were new in the sense that, when settled by Europeans, an indigenous culture and society was either nonexistent or was soon to be decimated. The societies which emerged, therefore, were ones unencumbered by persisting aspects of a previous social structure. What did influence the organization of such societies were primarily the concerns and interests of the European settlers. These, in turn, were shaped by the planters' ability to market tropical or semi-tropical staples in Europe, and by the production requirements associated with climate, existing technology and the need to gain access to an adequate labor force.

It was the latter which was in fact the central problem facing the planters and the leaders of these societies. There was an ample and growing opportunity to market sugar.[3] But the technology associated with sugar's cultivation and harvesting was labor intensive. This meant that if the planters were to be able fully to exploit the market opportunities available to them, they would require access to workers in much larger numbers than were locally available. Reliance on a domestic labor market for their labor supply was therefore an unattractive alternative. So too was participation in an international labor market since free immigration would have necessitated a bidding up of wage rates to levels which would have severely constrained output.[4] To produce in large volume, as the planters desired to do, therefore meant finding a means whereby workers would be made available to the plantations through some mechanism other than a free labor market.

Slavery was the classic institution through which this was done. The coercion, force, and violence which were at the core of slavery thus were central to the plantation's commercial success. Despite its immorality, there does not seem to be any doubt that slavery was successful in its intended function. In the only calculation of its kind, Fogel and Engerman have estimated that for cotton plantations in the Southern United States "...the application of force made it possible to obtain labor from slaves at less than half the price than would have had to have been offered in the absence of force."[5] A comparable cost advantage undoubtedly was the case in the Caribbean production of sugar as well.

At the very core of slavery was denial of occupational choice. Emancipation — achieved in the British West Indies in 1838 with the exception of Antigua where freedom was accomplished in 1834 — represented therefore a promise to the slaves and a threat to the planters. It seemed to imply that planters would no longer be able unilaterally to dictate employment conditions to plantation laborers. For freedom to be substantive in this way, however, would require the planters to participate in a labor market in which alternative income earning opportunities were available to the labor force. To possess real content, freedom required that choice in employment be available to the former slaves. Indeed, to a great extent the shape of the post-slave society would be determined precisely by the degree to which such options in employment became available to the former slaves. To the extent that a redress in that denial of opportunities occurred, the society would be transformed. As Woodville K. Marshall writes, "the legislation which ended slavery hinted at momentous, probably revolutionary changes in Caribbean society."[6]

Only to a limited extent was this promise fulfilled. The range of alternative employment opportunities which became available to the West Indies labor force with freedom remained very narrow. In certain locations, such as Guyana and Trinidad, that range was wider than in other territories such as St. Kitts and Barbados. The difference lay in the fact that in the former it was possible for the ex-slaves to become subsistence farmers. In the latter that alternative did not emerge.

The long standing consensus explanation of this pattern was that it was dictated by the land/labor ratio present in each location. Marshall traces this hypothesis to the 1841 writings of Herman Merivale who divided the region into three groupings: small heavily populated islands, larger islands like Jamaica, and thinly populated territories including Dominica as well as Guyana and Trinidad. But Marshall questions whether the land/labor ratio is itself a sufficient base upon which to explain post-emancipation settlement patterns. He insists that in addition to the basic demographic context, "the power of elite groups" in setting land sale policy should not be ignored. In this, Marshall endorses the work of Michel-Rolph Trouillot and Nigel Bolland who have called for more nuanced empirical studies than occurs when the land/labor ratio is mechanically applied.[7]

In fact there is not a statistically significant relationship between the land/labor ratio in the region and changes in sugar production between the mid-1820s and the mid-1840s.[8] The data in Table 1 thus do not provide support for the standard hypothesis according to which production least declined in the territories of greatest population density because the absence of available land precluded the former slaves from leaving the estates. It is true that the three territories with the lowest land/labor ratios, Antigua, Barbados and St. Kitts, all saw production rise in this period. But the increase in sugar production in Trinidad is flatly contradictory of the standard hypothesis. Elsewhere the ratio does not reliably predict variations in the pattern of sugar production trends.

What this suggests it that though the land/labor ratio undoubtedly was of relevance, it was not the sole or even a decisive determinant of labor force mobility and the post-emancipation trend in sugar production. Obviously population density was important in establishing the context in which emancipation was essayed. Nonetheless, other factors such as the pattern of land ownership and land sales policy were also pertinent. As Hugh Tinker puts it with regard to Barbados, it was possible to bond most of the former slaves to

Table 1

**Land–Labor Ratios and Changes in Sugar Production
Prior to and After Emancipation**

	Land/labor ratio	Percentage change sugar production 1824/33 to 1839/46
Antigua	3.1	+8.7
Barbados	1.7	+5.5
St. Kitts	2.9	+3.8
Trinidad	47.7	+21.7
British Guiana	832.4	−43.0
Dominica	16.3	−6.4
St. Lucia	15.5	−21.8
Nevis	5.0	−43.1
Montserrat	4.6	−43.7
St. Vincent	5.7	−47.3
Tobago	8.8	−47.5
Jamaica	12.2	−51.2
Grenada	6.3	−55.9

Source: S. L. Engerman, "Economic Change and Contract Labour in the British Caribbean: The End of Slavery and the Adjustment to Emancipation," in David Richardson (ed.), *Abolition and Its Aftermath: The Historical Context, 1790–1916* (London: Frank Cass and Company, Ltd., 1985), Table 2, p. 238.

the plantations because "though people might be free — the land remained in bondage."[9]

Rather than the conventional argument that the "pull" of peasant agriculture induced the movement off of the estates, Douglas Hall has suggested that living conditions on the estates after emancipation actually drove the freed people from them. Hall writes that the planters in the aftermath of emancipation and apprenticeship sought to bind the ex-slaves to the estates. They attempted to do so in one of two ways. Hall writes that the planters "either imposed high rents on houses and provision grounds, or they insisted that continued occupation would only be allowed if the occupants worked daily on the estates."[10] The planters, that is, sought to forestall the emergence of a competing small farm sector by curtailing the mobility of the former slaves. High rents were intended to increase the newly freed farmers' need for money wages and hence for work on the plantations. Continued occupancy was similarly a strategy to ensure plantation work.

Particularly in territories where uncultivated land was available this strategy was wrong-headed. In places such as Guyana and Jamaica, farming off of the plantations was a real option for the former slaves. In such a context it was necessary for the planters to make estate work more, not less, attractive if there was any hope that free workers would continue to labor on sugar plantations. Yet the approach adopted on the estates was precisely the contrary. The thought seems to have been that the planters would not have to compete with the small farm sector, but rather could bully the former slaves into accepting conditions of work contrary to their own interests. The planters, that is, thought they could introduce a new slavery system, but without the juridical support essential for a slave regime. Under the circumstances, as Hall puts it, "the reactions of the ex-slaves were immediate and from our vantage point, predictable."[11] By 1842 a substantial movement off of the estates was underway. In Jamaica in 1845 almost 20,000 persons held farms of ten acres or less and in Guyana about 22,000 acres were cultivated by about 4,000 freeholders.[12]

The loss of labor was not the only threat to the plantation sugar industry. It further was jeopardized by the Sugar Acts of 1846 and 1848 which removed the preferential tariff protection West Indian sugar received in the British market. At almost the same time a commercial crisis in Britain in 1847 involved and forced into bankruptcy several firms with interests in the West Indian sugar industry.[13] Thus it is that Dennis Benn writes that "the labour problem against the background of economic depression in the sugar industry...raised serious questions about the survival of the West Indian plantation economy."[14]

The fact is, however, that with important exceptions, the region's sugar industry successfully confronted these threats. In Barbados output more than doubled between the 1840s and 1860s. In Demerara (British Guiana), Trinidad and St. Kitts sugar production increased by more than 50 percent over these years and even St. Vincent and Antigua saw sugar output expand. To be sure Grenada and Jamaica experienced declines. But, in as much as

Table 2

Changes in Cane Sugar Production, 1839/46–1857/66

	Percentage change in annual production
Barbados	132.0
Demerara	92.5
Trinidad	77.1
St. Kitts	59.5
Antigua	12.2
St. Vincent	8.1
Grenada	–7.2
Jamaica	–24.7
Total British West Indies and Guiana	45.4
World	56.4

Source: Derived from Philip Curtin, "The British Sugar Duties and West Indian Prosperity," in Hilary Beckles and Verne Shepherd (eds.), *Caribbean Freedom: Economy and Society from Emancipation to the Present* (Kingston, Jamaica: Ian Randle Publishers, 1993), Table 4, p. 317.

regional sugar production grew by 45.4 percent in this period, it is clear that this was not a period of devastation for the region's sugar industry (Table 2).

The sugar industry in these years was helped by the fact that even with the passage of the Sugar Acts the relatively unprocessed muscovado sugar which dominated the region's exports was not as heavily taxed as more processed sugar. Further as indicated in Table 3 the thirty years between the early 1850s and 1880s saw relative stability in the price received for sugar. This meant that increased output could be achieved by those plantations which were successful in lowering their production costs. But what was fundamental to the survival of the sugar plantation economy was the power of public policy. Simply put, the plantation economy persisted because it was British policy

Table 3

Prices Received for West Indian Sugar in Great Britain, 1855/59–1910/14

Year	Shillings per hundred weight
1855–59	26.6
1860–64	22.6
1865–69	22.2
1870–74	24.2
1875–79	21.0
1880–83	20.2
1884–89	13.2
1890–94	13.1
1895–99	10.0
1900–04	9.3
1905–09	9.7
1910–14	11.0

Source: Calculated from Gisela Eisner, *Jamaica, 1830–1930: A Study in Economic Growth* (Manchester: Manchester University Press, 1961], Table XLIII, p. 244).

to see that it did. British colonial policy makers were fully aware of the crisis which faced plantation agriculture and from the early 1840s sought ways to ensure that it remained dominant in the region.

Fundamental in this regard was the colonial power's interest in assuring the estates of an abundant, low-cost labor force. Doing so required that labor's opportunity costs be kept low. For the plantations to be able to attract workers at the wage level they were prepared to pay, it was critical that alternative income-earning opportunities be minimized. In fact much of the effect of British policy was to assure that this was the case.

British policy in support of the estates' ability to attract workers at low wages took four forms. The purchase of land by small scale cultivators was purposefully made difficult. The Governor of Guyana in 1838 told that colony's Court of Policy, "If persons without capital will consider themselves entitled to demand land, let them not possess it without such restrictions as shall induce them to pause before they quit the more densely peopled regions for the interior."[15] Crown (government held) lands were often available only in lots in excess of the size the former slaves could afford and at per acre prices far beyond the means of the would-be farmers.[16] Second, very little public investment was undertaken to support the peasant sector which did emerge. Eisner writes that "what Jamaicans needed for agricultural development in the second half of the nineteenth century was roads, water supplies, agricultural research and extension services..." but none of these was undertaken on a sufficient scale: "...agricultural research and education suffered from lack of funds and poorly trained personnel."[17] Third, education in the region was neglected, a failing which could not help but constrain economic opportunities for the West Indian people. As reported in Table 4, illiteracy in the region was rampant. For most territories, data on this issue do not become available until 1911. Even so illiteracy, as reported by the population in response to census questions — a statistic which almost certainly understates illiteracy — was very high. In the larger territories of Guyana, Trinidad and Jamaica in 1911 about half of the people five years and older were unable to read and write. At an earlier date — Jamaica in 1871 — illiteracy was in excess of 80 percent.

Finally, indentured immigration was a critical element in the survival of plantation agriculture in Guyana and Trinidad, and to a lesser extent in Jamaica and elsewhere. Particularly in the former two locations, the importing of workers replaced the freed former slaves who in very large numbers no longer offered their services to the estates. In so doing immigration put downward pressure on wages in what otherwise would have been a market in which labor would have been scarce. Curtin writes that contract workers were paid at a rate "far below the market rate" and Brereton reports that in the 1860s in Trinidad "depression in the industry, and an ever-increasing labour supply, meant a reduction in the work-load and earnings of the resident labourers and a decline in the amount of work offered to non-resident workers."[18]

Large-scale immigration to the region was initiated in the mid and late 1840s. Between then and 1918 about 536,000 immigrants, almost all of whom according to the terms of their indenture were assigned to specific plantations, came to the West Indies. Of these about 300,000 came to Guyana, 157,000 to Trinidad and 54,000 to Jamaica. Of these immigrants, 80 percent came from India. The distribution of the migrants from the Subcontinent was similar to that of the migrants in general: 55.6 percent went

Table 4

Illiteracy Rates[1] in the Nineteenth Century: Selected West Indian Territories

Guyana 1911	56.3
Trinidad 1911	47.3
St. Lucia 1911	67.1
St. Vincent 1911	48.0
Antigua 1911	36.3
Montserrat 1911	31.8
St. Kitts, Nevis Anguilla 1911	32.8
Jamaica 1871	83.7
1881	77.1
1891	68.0
1911	52.8

[1]Persons unable to read and write minus population five and below as a percentage of population five and above.

Sources: Guyana: *Report of the Results of the Census of the Population 1911* by Geo. D. Bayley (Georgetown Demerara: The "Argosy" Co. Ltd., Printer to the Government of British Guiana, 1912); Trinidad: *Census of the Colony of Trinidad and Tobago 1911* (Trinidad: Printed at the Government Printing Office, Port of Spain, 1913); St. Lucia: *Report on the Census of the Island of Saint Lucia 1911* (Castries: Printed by the Government Printer at the Government Printing Office, 1912); St. Vincent: *St. Vincent, Reports and General Abstracts of the Census, 1911* (Kingstown: Printed at the Government Printing Office, 1911); Antigua: *Report on the Census of 1911 of Antigua and Its Dependencies* (St. John's: Government Printing Office, 1911); Montserrat: *Montserrat Census 1911, Report* (Barbados: Advocate Co. 1911); St. Kitts, Nevis Anguilla: *St. Kitts Nevis Census Report 1911* (NP: ND); Jamaica: *Census of Jamaica and Its Dependencies Taken on 4 April 1881* (Jamaica: Government Printing Establishment, 1882); *Census of Jamaica and Its Dependencies Taken on 6 April 1891* (Jamaica: Government Printing Office 1892); *Census of Jamaica and Its Dependencies, April 3 1911* (Jamaica: Government Printing Office, 1912).

to Guyana, 33.5 percent to Trinidad and 8.5 percent to Jamaica, with the others distributed in small numbers to the other islands.[19]

The general consensus in the historical literature is that these indentured immigrant workers were free only in a formal sense. Hugh Tinker referred to the whole system of state-sponsored migration as a "New System of Slavery", and Philip Curtin has agreed that "it certainly was a form of coerced labor — usually as unpleasant for the worker as slavery itself, but not identical to the old system." Recently Walton Look Lai described it as "not as extreme as chattel slavery, but certainly not free in the increasingly accepted metropolitan liberal sense of the term." Central to these judgements is the fact that once the immigrant had voluntarily agreed to a contract of indenture, his or her options were decisively limited. The immigrant was required to work on the specific plantation to which he or she was assigned and criminal penalties were applicable for breaches of work discipline on that estate. Movement beyond a two mile radius of that location was prohibited without permission from the plantation management. Lai writes that "this stringent pass-law system made the laborer a de facto prisoner of his specific plantation and was the major distinguishing mark of difference between an immigrant contract laborer and a free laborer."[20]

The cumulative effect of Government policy, then, was to constrain economic alternatives to plantation work. In the absence of more remunerative options, the former slaves and their descendants were under irresistible pressure to accept the low wages which the plantations offered. In this way plantation agriculture with its need for large numbers of low cost workers was permitted a continued existence. That continued existence, in its turn, limited the expansion of the small farm sector. Marshall, the principal historian of the West Indian peasantry writes:

> The revolution hardly got started. Blacks, as the militant industrial action clearly demonstrates did attempt during the first years of full freedom to realize their hopes and expectations; but, within ten years, a planter counter-revolution had successfully blocked most of the embryonic programme and had rendered precarious the existence of those institutions on which blacks had hoped to build.[21]

Only one national income accounts study is available to provide an extensive time series documenting the region's economic growth experience in this period.[22] In that study of Jamaica, however, the picture is clear (Table 5). As late as 1870 that country's gross domestic product per capita was lower than it had been in 1832 under slavery. Indeed in 1870 that statistic stood below the level reached in 1850, a year in which sugar still was experiencing the difficulties associated with emancipation. There is no doubt: economic

Table 5

Gross Domestic Product, Population and Gross Domestic Product per Capita, Jamaica, 1832, 1850, 1870, and 1890 (1910 pounds)

	Gross domestic product	Population	Gross domestic product per capita
1832	5,772,500	371,070[1]	15.6
1850	4,886,500	377,400[2]	12.9
1870	6,006,000	506,100[3]	11.9
1890	7,925,300	639,500[4]	12.4

[1]1834. [2]1844. [3]1871. [4]1891.

Sources: Calculated from Gisela Eisner, *Jamaica, 1830–1930: A Study in Economic Growth* (Manchester: Manchester University Press, 1961): Gross Domestic Product, Table 8.11, p. 119; Population, 1834, p. 127; 1850, 1871 and 1891, Table iv, p. 134.

modernization was not experienced in the West Indies in the nineteenth century.

The analytic issue to be confronted is whether the perpetuation of the plantation economy was responsible for the region's underdevelopment. In probably the most influential effort to explain Caribbean underdevelopment, George L. Beckford argues precisely that case. According to Beckford, since plantations were almost always owned by foreign corporations, they were responsible for substantial income leakages from the Caribbean. These losses, he believes represented a decisive constraint on West Indian economic development. Beckford writes that "foreign ownership results in the diminution of the surplus which becomes available for reinvestment.... Because of these leakages the development impact deriving from the multiplier effect is considerably dampened."[23] Indeed, Beckford writes that in contrast to the plantation sector, "the greatest potential for development resides in the peasant sector." This because it does not experience income leakages overseas and as a result better fosters internal markets than does the foreign based plantation sector. Beckford argues that what little development did occur in the nineteenth century had its origin in the peasantry. The growth of the small farm sector, he writes "led to a significant diversification of the economy and...a measure of independent economic development was achieved."[24]

Beckford's hypothesis, however, concerning the impact of foreign ownership on financial leakages has not been empirically validated. In her national income accounts study Eisner writes that she has "not been able to make estimates at all for profits sent abroad or other payments except for those made by public authorities."[25] As a result, numerous critics have remained agnostic about Beckford's view of the mechanisms of underdevelopment and particularly his thesis concerning the dynamism of the peasant sector.[26]

It is possible, however, to place plantation agriculture at the center of the region's development difficulties, and yet avoid Beckford's reliance on overseas leakages as the causal mechanism of underdevelopment. There are two dimensions to such an approach. The first concerns the consequences for productivity growth of low wages. The second addresses the stifling effect that support for plantation agriculture imposed on the non-plantation agricultural sector. Together, these combine to form a thesis which suggests that both the practice of plantation agriculture and the public support which that form of cultivation received served to limit the region's capability to achieve the kind of technological progress characteristic of modern economic growth.

Economic theory suggests that low wages encourage labor-intensive production methods. In turn, the limited use of capital in production means that output per worker tends to be low. Further, to the extent that improved methods of production are embodied in new capital equipment, the bias away from capital in production tends to depress the rate of productivity growth. Holding other factors constant, productivity growth will tend to be slower in a low wage setting than would be the case where higher wages resulted in a greater use of capital. As Hla Myint has written about plantations and mines, "their low wage policy induced them to use labour extravagantly, merely as an undifferentiated mass of 'cheap' or 'expendable' brawn-power. So, through the vicious circle of low wages and low productivity, the productivity of the indigenous labour even in the sparsely populated countries was fossilized at its very low initial level."[27]

The second dimension concerns the limitations which the support for plantation agriculture imposed on non-estate sectors of the economy. The British policy of constraining the development of non-plantation agriculture in the name of providing inexpensive labor to the estates had the effect of limiting the emergence of the kind of entrepreneurship essential for economic development. The West Indian people in their reaction to emancipation gave no evidence that market oriented behavior was antagonistic to their values and culture. Quite the contrary: the emergence of the peasantry despite official discouragement is testimony to their interest in commercial activity to raise their income levels. Yet the absence of public investment in research, infrastructure and education all meant that even when successful in becoming self-employed, very few Caribbean farmers were able to apply new productivity-raising techniques to production. Both the number of entrepreneurs and their productive competence was limited by the British policy of supporting the estates.

J.R. Ward, however, expresses doubts concerning this approach to explaining Caribbean underdevelopment. He dissents on three counts. Ward is skeptical that the incomes received by plantation workers in the Caribbean properly should be considered low. Furthermore, even if labor costs were low, he does not believe that low wages could have been an important impediment to Caribbean economic modernization. Finally Ward is at best agnostic concerning the British role in impeding non-estate agricultural development. That failure, he believes, could be attributable to causes other than British colonial policy. If so, support for even a weak plantation sector may have been the best of relatively poor alternatives. Thus Ward writes that "there are difficulties with this argument both on points of detail — how cheap was Caribbean labour by international standards and to what extent had sugar planters as a class eschewed innovation? — and also on its broader assumption that technical change was determined by the state of local labour markets."[28]

The first two issues — the level of real wages and the rate of innovation in sugar — are empirical questions. Insofar as the record is available, it seems clear that Ward's doubts are misplaced. Even if as almost certainly was the case agricultural wages were higher in the Caribbean than elsewhere, for example India, the importance of the point is not obvious. For the issue at hand is not a ranking of countries with regard to wage rates, but whether and to what extent the wages which West Indian agricultural workers had to settle for were sufficiently low so as to bias production techniques away from high capital labor ratios. If so, low wages can be said to have contributed to the slow pace of agricultural modernization.

There is direct evidence of wage levels in the Guyanese sugar industry. Guyana together with Trinidad was considered, in the region, a high wage economy. Nonetheless an investigating committee in 1871 made it clear that by no means did those wages result in anything but dire poverty.[29] Compensation for field work was by task. The pay for digging a twelve-foot trench, five feet deep was $0.80–$0.96; for digging a small drain, $0.05–$0.08 a rod;

for shovel plowing, \$2.80–\$3.50 an acre; for weeding, \$2.00–\$2.50 an acre; and for cane cutting about \$0.48 per acre. The commission calculated that on a typical plantation the average annual wage was \$57.31.

For the indentured workers, wages were even lower. The commission concluded that "it is evident that very few immigrant laborers average forty-eight cents a day for five days in a week." The commission estimated that only 44 percent of the indentured labor force earned more than the statutory minimum of \$1.20 per week and that a significant fraction earned less than this legal floor.

It is difficult to obtain data on the purchasing power of such wages. However, some indication of the level of poverty of the plantation workers is provided by comparing these income levels with the retail price of rice, a staple in the Guyanese diet. In 1872 a gallon of rice cost between \$0.24 and \$0.28. Thus a plantation worker earning \$1.20 per week, with no other source of income, and desiring to make no other purchases, was able to buy between four and five gallons of rice. There is no quantitative data available indicating the extent to which domestically grown ground provisions cultivated by the estate labor force supplemented such incomes. Impressionistic evidence, however, suggests that this additional source of income was widespread. Even so, it seems extremely unlikely that such supplemental income could have been large enough to invalidate the impression of destitution gained from the wage rate data. Thus there is ample basis for concluding that indeed the West Indies was a region in which wages were low.

Eisner provides data which permits the calculation of capital labor ratios in Jamaica's agricultural sector in the nineteenth century (see Table 6). It is unfortunate that no such estimate is available for a slave year. But Eisner's estimates do reveal that between 1850 and 1870 the capital output ratio actually declined by 5.4 percent. The 1890 capital output ratio was only 24.3 percent higher than it had been forty years earlier. Substantial increases in the capital intensity of Jamaican agriculture did not appear until after 1890. Reinforcing this impression of low levels of capital investment was Eisner's comment that "apart from increasing cane yields, improvements in cultivation were confined to the adoption of the plough. No method of mechanizing reaping was found and canes continued to be cut and cleaned manually."[30]

In light of this it is not a surprise to learn, also from Table 6, that productivity growth in Jamaican agriculture too was limited. Eisner's data show a very slow rate of growth of output per acre in sugar during the last half of the nineteenth century. The situation was even worse in the peasant sector. Eisner writes that "methods of cultivating food crops employed by the peasantry remained virtually unchanged throughout the century."[31] A similar pattern of productivity dualism almost certainly was present throughout the

Table 6

New Investment per Agricultural Worker, and
Sugar Production per Acre Jamaica, 1850–1910

	Investment[1] per worker[2]	Tons per acre
1850	284.0	0.74
1870	268.6	0.78
1890	353.0	0.80
1910	587.8	NA

[1]Durable producer goods. [2]Agricultural labor force for 1844, 1871, 1891 and 1911.

Source; Gisela Eisner, *Jamaica, 1830–1930.* Investment per worker calculated from Table XIX, p. 162, and Table LXIII, p. 308; tons per acre, Table LVIII, p. 294.

region. Productivity growth in the plantation sector was slow, but in the peasant sector it may have been nonexistent.

Despite Ward's skepticism, the empirical record does not contradict the hypothesis that it was plantation agriculture and the policies supportive of that form of agriculture which lay at the root of Caribbean underdevelopment. But to be convincing, this approach would have to establish that a hypothetical alternative to plantation dominance was viable. To indict plantation agriculture as the source of underdevelopment it, in short, is necessary to make the case that an alternative form of cultivation was feasible and could have achieved a higher rate of productivity growth than occurred on the plantations.

But what alternative could have been followed if the British had been less single-minded in their support of plantation agriculture? It is one thing to argue that public policies to maintain plantations were not instruments of modernization, but yet another to suggest that their support came at the expense of an alternative approach which better would have promoted economic modernization. Indeed, this precisely is the thrust of Ward's position when he asks "yet what were the practical possibilities for the development of a prosperous yeoman agriculture in the Caribbean during our period?" His answer is that such prospects were negligible. Ward writes, "it is fanciful to expect that the growing of yams or plantains on a tropical island would offer the same scope for the development of economic skills and the accumulation of capital as, for example, wheat farming in North America." Wheat in North America, according to Ward, "brought local processing requirements and opportunities for long-distance marketing" which ground provisions in the Caribbean were unable to do. Affirming the income generating capabilities of international trade, he concludes that "the Caribbean has gained more than it has lost by participation in the international economy, even through plantation agriculture, although the margin of advantage may have been narrower than for some other parts of the world."[32]

The problem with this is that though he shows the need to specify an alternative to the plantation system, Ward in pointing to the peasant cultivation of ground provisions is identifying a part of the plantation system itself. For as we have seen, independent peasant agriculture was discouraged by British policy. The small farm sector that did emerge was tolerated only to the extent that it was supportive of the plantation system. This it did by allowing labor to subsist until it was needed as a supplementary labor force at times of peak labor demand.[33] Where small scale farming existed it served as a useful source of supplemental income, but it was not an alternative to an economic way of life with the plantation at its center. Though Ward is right that it is necessary to make explicit an alternative to plantation agriculture before the latter can be criticized as failing to promote Caribbean prosperity, he has not specified properly what that hypothetical alternative could have been.

The issue at hand is not what crop or crops an alternative farm sector would have produced. The critical subject is whether an alternative farm structure could have been organized in which the incentives and capacities to be technologically progressive would have been greater than in the plantation economy. Could, in short, British policies have nurtured a class of West Indian farmers who would have developed the skills and learned the techniques of modern farming? Yams and plantains are not the problem. What is important is whether the productive capacities of Caribbean farmers could have been advanced so that the agricultural sector in the region would have become efficient and profitable.

Seen in this perspective, the tragedy of this period is that such an alternative was not even considered by the British. When in the aftermath of Emancipation a new peasant sector did struggle to make an appearance it was met with hostility by the Government. Though Ward does not acknowledge it, United States farmers could not have achieved the productivity they experienced without Government support in activities ranging from generous land distribution programs to support for productivity growth.[34] The same could have been true for Caribbean agriculturalists. Indeed, both W.A. Lewis and Eisner bemoan the fact that the kind of aid agriculture received in the United States was not made available to West Indian farmers. Lewis laments the fact that very little public investment in "irrigation, reclamation, drainage, terracing, conservation, afforestation and feeder roads" ever occurred in the region and Eisner explains that the peasants "were left to themselves to experiment with different crops and techniques."[35] Without such public investment, the emergence of a modern indigenous agricultural sector was not possible.

No one can be certain that a pattern similar to the one which emerged in the United States would have proved viable in the Caribbean. In light of the historical experience, however, it does seem reasonable that the burden of proof falls on the skeptics. Public policy in both locations was decisive for the pattern which emerged: family farms in the United States and estates in the Caribbean. Thus it is likely that if British policy had been to nurture a family farm agricultural sector in the West Indies, it could have been done. The reason it did not is quite clear: the Colonial Office did not believe that the West Indian people were capable of such a development-promoting alternative. The policy that was adopted consistently maintained that plantation agriculture, owned and managed by Europeans, was essential in the region. Without it, it was thought, the West Indies would economically collapse.

Critical in this regard was colonial policy in the 1840s, in the immediate aftermath of Emancipation. The tone was set in the work of two parliamentary commissions. The first, a parliamentary Select Committee, was appointed in 1842 to look into the deteriorating conditions in the region. According to this committee the problem was that plantation labor had grown increasingly scarce and expensive. To rectify this, it recommended that planters not offer land for sale to the former slaves, that immigration to the region be encouraged, and that squatting on abandoned land and on Crown Lands be eliminated. Thus, according to Lobdell, "the Committee accepted the argument that in many West Indian colonies the prosperity of estate agriculture had been and would be threatened by a general shortage of wage labor, the root cause of which was the growth of small settler and peasant cultivation."[36]

A second committee was appointed in the aftermath of the region's loss of its protected market in Great Britain. This committee's report in 1848 came to almost identical conclusions. It believed that the planters had been insufficiently compensated for the loss of their slaves. The estates therefore

suffered because emancipation had been "carried into effect without sufficient provision having been made for providing many of the Colonies with
an adequate command of free labour." In addition to repeating the recommendations of the 1842 committee that immigration be encouraged and
squatting controlled, this committee also believed that the region's sugar
should be granted a preferential tariff at least temporarily.[37]

These recommendations generally became policy when Lord Grey became the Colonial Secretary in 1846. Grey believed that:

> the highest interests of the Negroes required that the cultivation of sugar
> should not be abandoned and that the proprietors of European race should be
> enabled to maintain their present place in the society...which can only be
> done by giving them a greater command of labour.[38]

Grey argued that it was necessary to prevent:

> the abandonment of the colony by many of the inhabitants of European race,
> without whose assistance the remainder must speedily sink into barbarism.[39]

The former slaves, in short, could not take care of themselves. Support for
their efforts at development was out of the question.

It was British policy and the attitudes the British possessed with regard to
the people of the Caribbean that resulted in the survival of the plantation
economy. That economy, however, provided very little room for the structural
transformation which characterizes modern economic growth. The Caribbean people were not encouraged to become agents of technological advance; nor were they educated well enough to be able to be such agents, even
if encouraged. At root here was the belief by the colonial rulers that the
people of the region were simply not capable of becoming technically
competent. British policy, quite explicitly, saw ruin ahead unless British
estate owners provided low skill agricultural work for the West Indian
people. With policies in place to achieve that end, the plantation economy of
the West Indies survived Emancipation. But those policies also meant that
the region became a technological backwater. Because of them the West
Indies had no chance to experience the process of modern economic growth.

NOTES

1. Lloyd Best, "The Choice of Technology Appropriate to Caribbean Countries,"
   Working Papers, No. 15, July 1976, Centre for Developing Area Studies,
   McGill University, Montreal, Reprinted March 1979, p. 6.

2. Charles Wagley, "Plantation-America: A Culture Sphere," in Vera Rubin (ed.), *Caribbean Studies: A Symposium* (Seattle: University of Washington Press, 1960), p. 5.

3. See Sidney Mintz, *Sweetness and Power: The Place of Sugar in Modern History* (New York: Viking, 1985) for a discussion of the long-term growth in the demand for sugar.

4. Richard S. Dunn, *Sugar and Slaves: The Rise of the Planter Class in the English West Indies, 1624–1713* (Chapel Hill: The University of North Carolina Press, 1972), pp. 67–74.

5. Robert William Fogel and Stanley L. Engerman, *Time on the Cross: The Economics of American Negro Slavery* (Boston: Little, Brown and Company, 1974), I, p. 238.

6. Woodville K. Marshall, "'We Be Wise to Many More Tings': Black Hopes and Expectations of Emancipation," in Hilary Beckles and Verene Shepherd (eds.), *Caribbean Freedom: Society and Economy from Emancipation to the Present* (Kingston Jamaica: Ian Randle Publishers, 1993), p. 12.

7. Woodville K. Marhsall, "The Post-Slavery Labour Problem Revisited," *The 1990 Elsa Goveia Memorial Lecture* (Mona, Jamaica: Department of History, The University of the West Indies, 1991), pp. 3–5.

8. The r^2 for the data in Table 1 is 0.0323. When Guyana is removed and with it the distorting effects of its land size, the r^2 remains statistically not significant at 0.1598.

9. Hugh Tinker, *A New System of Slavery: The Export of Indian Labour Overseas, 1830–1920* (London: Oxford University Press, 1974), p. 2.

10. Douglas Hall, "The Flight from the Estates Reconsidered: The British West Indies, 1838–1842," in Hilary Beckles and Verene Shepherd (eds.), *Caribbean Freedom*, p. 59.

11. Ibid., p. 60.

12. Woodville K. Marshall, "Peasant Development in the West Indies Since 1838," in Hilary Beckles and Verene Shepherd (eds.), *Caribbean Freedom*, p. 101.

13. Gisela Eisner, *Jamaica, 1830–1930: A Study in Economic Growth* (Manchester: Manchester University Press, 1961), pp. 198–199.

14. Denis Benn, *The Growth and Development of Political Ideas in the Caribbean, 1774–1983* (Mona, Kingston, Jamaica: Institute of Social and Economic Research, University of the West Indies, 1987), p. 35.

15. Quoted in Jay R. Mandle, *The Plantation Economy: Population and Economic Change, 1838–1960* (Philadelphia: Temple University Press, 1973), p. 22.

16. Michael J. Craton, "Reshuffling the Pack: The Transition from Slavery to Other Forms of Labor in the British Caribbean, ca. 1790–1890," in *New West Indian Guide*, Vol. 68, no. 1/2 (1994), p. 55.

17. Gisela Eisner, *Jamaica, 1830–1930*, pp. 316–317.

18. Philip Curtin, *The Rise and Fall of the Plantation Complex: Essays in Atlantic History* (Cambridge: Cambridge University Press, 1990), p. 176. Bridget Brereton, *A History of Modern Trinidad, 1783–1962* (Kingston and London: Heinemann Education Books Caribbean Ltd.: 1981), p. 106.

19. George Roberts and Joycelyn Byrne, "Summary Statistics on Indentured and Associated Migration Affecting the West Indies, 1834–1918, *Population Studies*, Vol. 20, No. 1 (1966) pp. 127, 129.

20. Hugh Tinker, *A New System of Slavery: The Export of Indian Labour Overseas, 1830–1920*; Philip Curtin, *The Rise and Fall of the Plantation Complex*, p. 76; Walton Look Lai, *Indentured Labor, Caribbean Sugar: Chinese and Indian Migrants to the British West Indies, 1838–1918* (Baltimore: The Johns Hopkins University Press, 1993), p. 62. See also Robert Miles, *Capitalism and Unfree Labour: Anomaly or Necessity?* (New York: Tavistock Publications, 1987), pp. 90–93.

21. Woodville K. Marshall, "'We Be Wise To Many More Tings'" p. 18.

22. There is one national accounts study for Guyana, but it includes only two data points, 1832 and 1852. See Michael Moohr, "The Economic Impact of Slave Emancipation in British Guiana, 1832–1852," *Economic History Review*, Vol. 24, no. 4 (1972), pp. 588–607.

23. George L. Beckford, *Persistent Poverty: Underdevelopment in Plantation Economies of the Third World* (New York: Oxford University Press, 1972), pp. 186, 187.

24. George L. Beckford, "Caribbean Rural Economy," in George L. Beckford (ed.), *Caribbean Economy* (Mona, Kingston, Jamaica: Institute of Social and Economic Research, University of the West Indies, 1975), pp. 86, 81.

25. Gisela Eisner, *Jamaica, 1830–1930*, p. 283.

26. See for example Dennis Pantin, "The Plantation Economy Model and the Caribbean," in *Bulletin*, Institute of Development Studies, University of Sussex, Vol. 12, no 1 (1980), pp. 17–23.

27. Hla Myint, *The Economics of the Developing Countries* (New York: Frederick A. Praeger, 1964), pp. 56–57.

28. J.R. Ward, *Poverty and Progress in the Caribbean, 1800–1960* (London: Macmillan, 1985), p. 53.

29. The following three paragraphs are based on Jay R. Mandle, *The Plantation Economy*, pp. 62–63.

30. Gisela Eisner, *Jamaica, 1830–1930*, p. 301.

31. Gisela Eisner, *Jamaica, 1830–1930*, p. 305.

32. J.R. Ward, *Poverty and Progress in the Caribbean*, pp. 64–65.

33. For a discussion of the emergence of rice and a discussion of these issues see Jay R. Mandle, "Population and Economic Change: The Emergence of the

Rice Industry in Guyana, 1895–1915," *The Journal of Economic History*, Vol. 30, no. 4 (December 1970).

34. Donald L. Winters, "The Economics of Midwestern Agriculture, 1865–1900," in Lou Ferleger (ed.), *Agriculture and National Development* (Ames: Iowa State University Press, 1990), pp. 76–77, 80–81.

35. W. Arthur Lewis, "Forward" in Gisela Eisner, *Jamaica, 1830–1930,* p. xxi, and Gisela Eisner, *Jamaica 1830–1930,* p. 225.

36. Richard A. Lobdell, "British Officials and the West Indian Peasantry, 1842–1938," in Malcolm Cross and Gad Heuman (eds.), *Labour in the Caribbean* (London: Macmillan Caribbean, 1988), p. 196.

37. *Eighth Report of the Select Committee on Sugar and Coffee Planting,* 29 May, 1848 (Parliamentary Papers, 1848, Vol. XXIII) as quoted in Lobdell, "British Officials and the West Indian Peasantry," pp. 197–198.

38. As quoted in Ibid., p. 198.

39. As quoted in Denis Benn, *The Growth and Development of Political Ideas in the Caribbean*, pp. 36–37.

CHAPTER 3

The Erosion of
Plantation Dominance

The combination of large-scale indentured immigration and the limiting of educational and occupational opportunities had permitted the West Indian plantation sugar industry successfully to survive the crisis associated with Emancipation. To be sure, these mechanisms of survival had been responsible for the fact that the region did not successfully experience essential elements of the process of economic modernization. Nonetheless, it is true, as Richard Lobdell points out that "between 1865 and 1883 a mild prosperity seems to have visited the West Indian sugar industry."[1]

But one thing which these mechanisms could not do was protect the sugar producers from changes in the world market for their product. And changes in that market by the last two decades of the century had become profound. As indicated in Table 1, European beet sugar production doubled between 1850 and 1860, nearly tripled between 1860 and 1870 and almost doubled again between 1870 and 1880. As a result of this growth in production, by the 1880s increases in the supply of sugar tended to exceed the growth in its demand on international markets. The result was a dramatic collapse in the price of sugar (see Table 3 of Chapter 2). Between the early 1880s and the mid-1890s sugar's price fell by more than fifty percent, a decline which could not help but have a devastating effect on the West Indian sugar industry.

Not surprisingly, the impact of sugar's price collapse was most damaging in the territories which were high cost producers. As indicated in Table 2, between 1884 and 1904 the last remnants of the sugar industry were destroyed in Dominica, Grenada and St. Vincent, while proportionately very

Table 1

European and World Production of Sugar, 1850–1910 (1000 tons)

Year	European production	World production	Europe as % of world
1850	159	1076	14.8
1860	332	1725	19.2
1870	939	2723	34.5
1880	1827	3832	47.7
1890	3399	5716	59.5
1900	5410	8385	64.5
1910	6074	12705	47.8

Source: Ph.G. Chalmin, "Important Trends in Sugar Diplomacy Before 1914," in Bill Albert and Adrian Graves (eds.), *Crisis and Change in the International Sugar Economy, 1860-1914* (Norwich and Edinburgh, ICS Press, 1984), Table 2.2, p. 10, and Table 2.3, p. 12.

large declines in output were experienced in Jamaica, St. Lucia and St. Kitts/Nevis. Elsewhere, falling production was experienced, though the magnitude of the decline in Antigua, Barbados, Guyana, and Trinidad and Tobago was not as great as elsewhere in the region. As a result of these trends, Guyana's claim to being the preeminent sugar producer in the region was strengthened. In the 1870s Guyana produced about one-third of West Indian sugar. In 1904 that fraction had increased to more than two-fifths.

The manufacturing stage of sugar production was the most capital intensive part of the production process. As a result, it was also the stage where technical efficiencies were concentrated. Guyana and Trinidad took the lead in this regard. In his detailed study of the region's sugar industry in the late nineteenth century, R.W. Beachy writes that the estates in Guyana were noted for their "utility, economy and manufacturing appliances."[2] But with the beet sugar crisis, advances in productivity slowed as investment in the West Indian industry declined. Lobdell writes that "improved factory operations helped reduce overall production costs after 1884 in both Guyana and

Table 2

West Indian Sugar Production (1000 tons)

	1870	1884	1894	1904	1914
Antigua	12	15	12	14	15
Barbados	38	60	59	56	30
Dominica	4	2	1	–	–
Grenada	4	2	0	0	0
Guyana	76	123	104	108	109
Jamaica	25	20	24	10	21
St. Kitts/Nevis	15	19	17	12	13
St. Lucia	6	9	5	5	4
St. Vincent	10	9	3	1	–
Trinidad/Tobago	44	64	47	46	56
Total	233	323	272	252	248

Source: Christian Schnakenbourg, "From Estate to Central Factory: The Industrial Revolution in the Caribbean (1840–1905)," in Bill Albert and Adrian Graves (eds.), *Crisis and Change in the International Sugar Economy 1860–1914* (Norwich and Edinburgh: ICS Press, 1984), Table 7.5, p. 93.

Trinidad," but that "capital investment in sugar industries of other British West Indian colonies virtually ceased after 1884."[3]

Despite the efficiencies of the Guyanese and Trinidadian industries, sugar in the West Indies did not experience rapid productivity growth. Data in this regard are scarce. But Tables 3 and 4 provide information on yields over time in Jamaica and Guyana. Both reveal a sluggish experience. In Jamaica there was virtually no increase in yields per acre between 1846 and 1890. It was only during the 1890s, when sugar production was in decline, that yields increased substantially. Similarly, in Guyana yields were stable between 1851 and 1871, and accelerated most rapidly only during the 1880s.

In reaction to their competitive losses to the subsidized European beet sugar industry, the region's cane growers pleaded with the Colonial Office for tariff protection. Instead, in 1883 a Royal Commission was appointed to investigate the deteriorating financial condition of the colonial governments

Table 3

**Sugar Output per Acre, Jamaica,
1846–96 (1000 tons)**

1846	0.74
1859	0.64
1870	0.78
1880	0.80
1890	0.80
1896	0.92
1929	1.91

Source: Gisela Eisner, *Jamaica, 1830–1930: A Study in Economic Growth* (Manchester: Manchester University Press, 1961), p. 294.

of the region. Richard Lobdell argues that it was in the report of this commission that the West Indian peasantry received its first official approval. This approbation occurred in the context of the Commission's discussion of the fact that increasingly the region's small farmers were involved in export agriculture. Even so, the Commission adopted a conventional pro-plantation agriculture stance. It complained that the region's estates were unable "to obtain at all times a reliable supply of labor," a failure which it attributed to "the natural indolence of the negro" and the availability of alternative employment opportunities. In its recommendation for continued support for indentured immigration, even in the context of the depressed sugar market, Lobdell concedes that "the Commission could not quite break away from the traditional view that peasant cultivation and estate agriculture were incompatible."[4]

Another Royal Commission was appointed in 1897 and this one more unambiguously supported the small farm sector. Its charge was to "enquire into the conditions and prospects of the sugar-growing Colonies in the West Indies and to suggest means calculated to restore and maintain the prosperity of those Colonies." The "special remedies or measures of relief" which the Commission unanimously endorsed were:

1) The settlement of the labouring population on small plots of land as peasant proprietors and 2) The establishment of minor agricultural industries

Table 4

Sugar Exports per Acre Under Cultivation, Guyana 1861–1931

Year	Area under cane (acres)	Exports (tons)	Exports per acre
1851	31,354	30,124	0.96
1861	52,726	50,643*	0.96
1871	75,944	72,943*	0.96
1881	77,379	92,323	1.19
1891	78,307	116,968	1.49
1901	67,884	105,694	1.56
1908	74,860	115,213	1.54
1921	63,420	108,270	1.71
1931	61,097	119,346	1.95

*Hogsheads converted to tons by multiplying by 0.7.

Source: Dwarka Nath, *A History of Indians in Guyana* (London: Published by the Author, second revised edition, 1970), Table 10, p. 249.

and the improvement of the system of cultivation, especially in the case of small proprietors.

The Commission acknowledged that "the settlement of the labourer on the land has not as a rule been viewed with favour in the past by the persons interested in sugar estates." It went on, "what suited them best was a large supply of labourers, entirely dependent on being able to find work on the large estates and consequently subject to their control and willing go to work at low rates of wages." The Commission declared that "the negro is an efficient labourer, especially when he receives good wages." However, it also asserted that these individuals were "disinclined to continuous labour extending over a long period of time" and often are "unwilling to work if the wages offered are low." All of this, combined with the fact that "the negroes like to own land by which they may make their livelihood and take a pride in the position as landholders," led the Commission to the conclusion that "no reform offers so good a prospect for permanent welfare in the future of the West Indies as the settlement of the labouring population on the land as small peasant proprietors."[5]

Yet the Commission did not call for the dismantling of the plantation system. Instead it argued "whilst we think that the Governments of the different colonies should exert themselves in the direction of facilitating the settlement of the labouring population on the land, we see no objection to the system of large estates where they can be maintained under natural economic conditions." It concluded that "in many places they afforded the best, and sometimes the only profitable means of cultivating certain products and that it is not impossible for the two systems of large estate and peasant holdings, to exist side by side with mutual advantage."[6] To this end, the Commission recommended that a Department of Economic Botany be established for the Windward and Leeward Islands in order to sponsor research on improved cultivation techniques. It also advocated public subsidies for a steamship line in order to open markets for the region's small farmers. Finally, it recommended that grants-in-aid be provided for roads, land settlement, and the paying off of accumulated government debt and current deficits.[7]

While the Commission did not believe that a choice was required between the plantation and peasant sectors, its Secretary, Sydney Olivier, did. In a confidential memorandum, Olivier wrote that "so far as the negro and negroid population of these Colonies is concerned, the estate system of sugar production is either unworkable or oppressive and conducive to retrogression rather than to progress." He wrote that the government should not commit itself to preserving estate agriculture, but rather should undertake a policy only "to break its fall."[8]

The Colonial Secretary, however, agreed with the Commission that the plantation sugar industry should not be sacrificed in the name of the peasantry. While supporting the establishment of a system of small land holdings, Joseph Chamberlain insisted in a circular to the region's governors that support for small farmers should be "pursued with due regard to the maintenance of the sugar industry, and in such a manner as not to withdraw from estates those who are under contract to work upon them."[9]

But not only did Chamberlain side with the Commission on the issue of the plantation versus the peasant sector. He, at least initially, rejected all of the Commission's proposals concerning the establishment of alternative industries and the provision of financial support for the region's peasantry. Chamberlain's goal was to help the West Indies' sugar industry by negotiating the removal of the bounties which supported the European beet industry. His position was that the British should use the threat of countervailing tariffs as a negotiating tool to secure that goal. Aside from that, he confined himself to agreeing with the Commission to pay off the public debt of the smaller islands. In a paper submitted to the Cabinet, Chamberlain argued that in taking steps to eliminate European sugar bounties, "we clear ourselves of our principle responsibility." He went on, "If after this the colonies cannot live, at least it is not our fault."[10]

H.A. Will finds Chamberlain's cool reaction to the recommendation to promote alternative industries "puzzling" in light of Chamberlain's "commitment to development." Will writes that in abstaining from new economic initiatives, Chamberlain was "perhaps bowing reluctantly to political and financial necessity." But, Will goes on, "he also seems to have lacked confidence in the success of the alternative or so called 'minor' industries." In this, Will assigns responsibility primarily to Chamberlain's advisors, particularly C.P. Lucas, the head of the West Indian department in the Colonial Office. According to Will, "they [the advisors] viewed with concern any decrease in the resident white or Indian immigrant population of the West Indies which might follow a decline of the sugar industry." Will notes that "such considerations seem to have led Chamberlain and his advisers to the view that the future of the West Indian colonies depended primarily on its revival."[11] Thus despite official rhetoric in support of the small farm sector, in point of fact official policy never did fully endorse a restructuring of the region's agricultural sector. Neither the providing of technical assistance to the farmers, nor the construction of infrastructure in rural areas, much less an extensive land reform program, became part of official colonial policy. Thomas C. Holt concludes that "racist ideology and the politics it produced explain much of the anomalous contradiction between the rhetoric and performance of the peasantry's 'new deal.'"[12]

Despite the unwillingness of the Colonial Office to envision a West Indian future without estate domination, the beet sugar crisis signalled the beginning of the end of the region's plantation economy. The collapse of sugar prices triggered defensive responses by both the West Indian labor force and plantation management. These responses, in turn, meant that the long era in which planters were able to produce sugar profitably by utilizing masses of workers in manual labor began to draw to a close. Though the crisis was finally resolved in 1902 when the European subsidy system was abolished, it had revealed to the planters that low wages alone were not sufficient to ensure profits. Furthermore as the 1897 Commission noted, the decline in wages which already had occurred since the onset of falling sugar prices meant that "further reductions of salaries or wages was impracticable."[13] Estate workers, in the meantime, reacted to the crisis with an intensified search for alternative employment. This took the form of efforts at land settlement or emigration to higher paying occupations elsewhere in the Caribbean. Thus the basis of the plantation economy — the estates' demand for large numbers of unskilled workers, a demand which was satisfied by employees with few alternative work options — began to unravel in the last two decades of the nineteenth century.

Where sugar remained an important industry in the West Indies, a noticeable change in trend in productivity growth occurred. In contrast to the relative stability which prevailed throughout most of the period since mid-century, yields per acre in the Jamaican sugar industry more than doubled between 1896 and 1929 (see Table 3). Similarly in Guyana yields improved dramatically between 1908 and 1931 (see Table 4). Higher yielding varieties of cane were an important source of this improvement in productivity though there were as well continuing advances in manufacturing efficiency. Even in field operations, where methods of production changed least, employment grew proportionately less than did output. Especially in the years after World War I, as the West Indian Royal Commission reported in 1938, "a big reduction in the costs of production ... has enabled the industry to supply a steadily increasing quantity of sugar to the British consumer at a falling price."[14]

In making recommendations partially in support of the peasantry, the 1897 Royal Commission was endorsing a process already underway. Woodville Marshall, the principal historian of the West Indian peasantry, describes the period between the 1850s and 1900 as one of consolidation "during which there was continuing expansion of the number of peasants and more important a marked shift by the peasants to export crop production."[15] At the same time, however, the unwillingness of Joseph Chamberlain's Colonial Office to break with plantation dominance is illustrative of Sidney Mintz's point that "the peasants of the Caribbean have been embattled since their beginnings.... Traditionally, any kind of agricultural or infrastructural improvement — in roadways, marketing facilities, agricultural extension and credit, crop varieties, etc. — went to the plantation sector rather than the peasant sector." Indeed, Mintz concludes that "perhaps the most unusual thing about Caribbean peasantries is that any of them survived at all; but so they have."[16]

Nowhere was this process more dramatic than in Jamaica. There, the small farm sector found in bananas an export crop which both possessed a relatively strong market and was within the resource and technical competence of the colony's small farmers.[17] But this phenomenon was not confined to Jamaica. In the Windward Islands as sugar declined, peasant export activity increased. Among the crops shipped abroad from St. Vincent, Grenada, St. Lucia and Dominica were arrowroot, cotton, spices, cocoa, citrus, bananas, logwood, and sugar.[18]

Cocoa was the crop of choice for small farmers in Trinidad and this too became an important export product. There, newly sold public or Crown Land formed the basis of the new industry, unlike the situation in Jamaica where private land sales were the source of the small farm sector. Two different organizational forms were present in Trinidadian cocoa. In one case, direct purchases of Crown Lands were made by small holders. Thus between 1875 and 1885 over 54,000 acres were sold in lots which averaged about sixteen acres each. Farmers would plant and tend to cocoa trees on these holdings. When the trees matured, the land was sold typically to large land owners to be incorporated in their cocoa estates. The alternative and probably dominant organization form was a contract system. In this, small farmers would agree to tend to the trees on a unit of land owned by the estate planters. While doing so the small farmers would be free to cultivate crops on unused land. When the trees started to bear, payment on a per tree basis was made to the cultivator who then moved onto a new holding and repeated the process.

Throughout the last quarter of the nineteenth century, the market for cocoa was strong. As a result, as Bridget Brereton writes, "for the Trinidad peasantry, cocoa provided a profitable export crop that required neither considerable outlays of capital nor a large labour force." But Brereton emphasizes that this relative prosperity experienced by the Trinidadian peasantry occurred despite the fact that "the attitude of the government towards them tended to remain indifferent or even hostile."[19]

In Guyana the crisis in sugar resulted in the emergence of rice as a peasant crop.[20] Indentured immigration had continued in the Colony during the 1890s even though sugar exports were in decline and there was a fall in the demand for sugar estate workers. The crisis in sugar, however, had triggered an increase in East Indian repatriation. Both the colonial government and the sugar industry stood in opposition to this increased propensity to return to India. Immigrants, even after their period of indenture had expired, acted as a supplementary labor force for the sugar estates. In an attempt to dissuade immigrants from returning home, the government moved to ease the terms of purchase of Crown Lands and established Land Settlement Schemes on three former sugar estates. A substantial increase in the colony's village population resulted which, in turn, permitted a new rice industry to emerge in the mid-1890s. The new industry was almost entirely composed of small-scale East Indian producers. Growth in output was rapid, so that within about ten years, rice imports had been eliminated and by about 1910 Guyanese rice had found an export market in neighboring West Indian colonies.

Throughout the region, then, as Woodville Marshall writes, "peasant activity modified the character of the original pure plantation economy and society."[21] In widening the range of crops produced in the region, it was the peasant sector which was the source of innovation. Nevertheless, official policy was ambivalent, officially supportive but stinting in practice. Despite rhetoric to the contrary, the peasants were, in Gisela Eisner's words, "left to themselves to experiment with different crops and techniques."[22] As a result, the peasant's ability to transform the structure of the West Indies economy was limited because of insufficient resources, knowledge and research.

The hegemony of plantation agriculture was eroded by one other mechanism aside from productivity growth and the emergence of a peasantry. From the mid-1890s, a new form of emigration made its appearance. In the past, population movements in the West Indies had largely been confined to the region and in response to estate labor demand. In locations where the demand for labor was high relative to its supply, the resulting comparatively high wage paid to estate labor attracted immigrants. Thus Trinidad and Guyana attracted substantial numbers of workers from the islands of the Eastern Caribbean. But from the 1880s, migration took on a wider geographic scope. Industries other than sugar were involved and destinations other than the English-speaking West Indies attracted migrants from the region. For the first time people from the West Indies emigrated to find work in Cuba, the Dominican Republic, Bermuda and the United States. The Republic of Panama too was an important destination for West Indian migrants. The movement of construction workers for the canal project there occurred in a series of waves, the first between 1850 and 1855, the second between 1880 and 1894 and the third after 1904. These surges were associated with phases of the construction of the canal and supporting infrastructure. In general, most of the industries attracting West Indian migrants in this period were the result of United States business investment. Thus it is that Dawn Marshall writes that "although only a small proportion of the actual movements were to the United States itself, they were certainly movements in search of the 'yankee dollar.'"[23] Data on the size of this emigration are unreliable, though Marshall estimates that net emigration from the West Indies totalled 130,000 during the period between 1885 and 1920, the majority of whom were from Jamaica and Barbados.[24]

By the turn of the century or the early decades of the new century, the range of employment options available to the West Indian labor force had widened in two directions. The expanding peasant sector had created at least part-time non-plantation work in agriculture. In addition, expanding geographic mobility provided West Indian workers with work outside of the confines of the region. As a result, the plantations' overwhelming dominance in the fabric of West Indian life was not quite as oppressive as it once had been. The estates were no longer virtually the sole source of employment in the region. No longer was it true, as it had been both under slavery and in the five or six decades subsequent to Emancipation that the planters could single-handedly dictate the shape of economic life. Alternatives had appeared.

But to say that the domination of the plantation sector had been eroded is not, however, to argue that the plantation economy had as yet been dismantled. In the larger territories — Jamaica, Trinidad, Guyana and Barbados — plantation agriculture continued to dominate. No longer did the estates necessarily specialize in sugar. Cocoa in Trinidad and bananas in Jamaica had become plantation crops. Large-scale export agriculture had considerably been reduced in importance in locations such as Grenada, Dominica and St. Vincent. Yet land ownership, even there, remained highly concentrated in large units.

The problem was that though the scope of options for the West Indian labor force had widened, an alternative growth-promoting set of institutions had yet to appear in the region. The plantation economy — the structure which had at once brought the West Indies into the world economy but at the same time constrained its economic modernization — was no longer the sole basis upon which the West Indian economy and society was constructed. But official lack of support meant that the peasant sector clearly was subordinate to it and did not represent an alternative structure upon which to build a modern economy. Manufacturing was not even conceived of as an option for the region. Emigration was a rational individual response to labor market circumstances, but hardly represented a means by which to modernize the West Indian economy. Thus though the early decades of the twentieth century saw the ending of the all but total economic domination of labor-intensive and large-scale agriculture, an alternative, growth-promoting economic structure was not constructed.

In this context, a new problem, the threat of involuntary unemployment, appeared for the first time. Surplus labor had never been an issue in the Caribbean. Always in the past an increase in the region's population had been warmly welcomed by the planters and colonial administrators. More people meant more plantation workers, and that, given the sugar industry's labor intensive production methods, meant more output and profits. Where labor shortages threatened, in Trinidad and Guyana, indentured immigration had produced very high rates of population growth, an expansion which provided the estates of those territories with the plentiful labor supply their plantation agriculture required. But in the years subsequent to the beet sugar crisis, the regional industry had increasingly turned to productivity growth as a means of achieving its growth targets. Sugar could no longer absorb virtually unlimited supplies of labor. This attention to labor productivity growth occurred as the region entered a new era in its demographic history. It was in this period that, for the first time, the birth rate in the West Indies tended to exceed the death rate. It also occurred at a time when, because of the completion of the Panama Canal and the onset of the Great Depression, opportunities for emigration were considerably reduced. The result was that, for the first time, there was a threat that the region's labor force would be in excess of the absorptive power of the region's economy. The tragedy was profound. Now that the health of the West Indian people had improved to the point where they could expand their numbers, it turned out that the resulting increase in the population and labor force was not needed on the estates. This failure came at a heavy cost. Not only would the region continue to be denied modern growth; but also for the first time the Caribbean was required to face the problem of unemployment.

This new era in the region's demographic experience can be dated from the mid- or late 1920s. Mortality in the West Indies peaked in 1918 and 1919 because of the worldwide influenza epidemic which visited the region in that year. Thus, death rates skyrocketed in Guyana from a level of about 24.0 per 1000 of the population in 1913 and 1914 to 41.0 in 1918. By the mid-1920s this mortality measure had subsided back to about 24.0 and continued in the range of 24.0 to about 26.0 until 1929. In that year the death rate in Guyana fell to 23.0 and continued to fall consistently in the years thereafter. By 1935 the death rate had dropped to 20.3 and five years later it had fallen to 18.1.[25] With Guyana's birth rate ranging narrowly at about 32.0 throughout the 1920s and 1930,[26] the colony for the first time experienced natural population growth (an excess of births over deaths) which by the end of the 1930s came to almost 1.5% per year. A very similar pattern appeared on the Western side of the region in Jamaica. Death rates peaked between 1916–20, declined in 1921–25 to the level experienced before the flu pandemic and then noticeably fell in the late 1920s. As a result, in Jamaica, like Guyana, population growth in the early 1930s already had increased to about 1.5 percent per year.[27] This pattern, experienced widely in the region, meant, as Dawn Marshall writes that "the resultant natural increase caused concern from early in the 20th century."[28]

Only limited study has been done to account for the mortality decline which occurred in these years. Marshall writes that "it was due to a number of reasons including very large declines in infant and child mortality; the introduction from overseas of health measures like DDT control and possibly also the improvement of socio-economic conditions."[29] In Guyana a similar conclusion seems warranted. It appears that improvements in the water supply, methods of disposing of waste, the colony's medical facilities and an increase in the distribution of information concerning pre- and postnatal care all contributed to declining morality.[30]

What is clear is that the population growth of the twentieth century occurred in a far different context than that of the previous century. Where in the past, immigration meant an expanded productive capability in sugar, now with the labor absorbing capacity of sugar curtailed, and with emigration reduced, the region entered an era in which for the first time, the supply of labor exceeded its demand.

To this combustible mix of increasing unemployment and a slowing of emigration was added in the late 1920s and 1930s a deterioration in the markets for West Indian sugar and bananas. The price of exports from the West Indies declined by almost 50 percent between 1928 and 1933. As a result, according to Arthur Lewis, "workers were forced to submit to drastic wage cuts, increased taxation and unemployment." This proved to be too much. Writing in 1938 Lewis argued that "had there existed constitutional machinery for the redress of grievances, there might well have been no upheavals." But such ameliorating institutions were not present in the region since, according to Lewis "government and employers have always been hostile to collective bargaining and the political constitution is deliberately framed to exclude the workers from any control over the legislature."[31] The result was a series of strikes, riots and semi-insurrections which spread through the region during the years 1934–38.

From this instability emerged both the rise of trade unions and the entry of workers into West Indian politics. And with those two developments the final nail in the coffin of the plantation economy was hammered into place. A plantation economy requires a dependent labor force, one which is unable to threaten successfully to undertake collective action. Precisely because trade unions give a voice to workers, the riots of the 1930s produced what Arthur Lewis described as the "1930s social revolution."

NOTES

1. Richard A. Lobdell, "Patterns of Investment and Sources of Credit in the British West Indian Sugar Industry, 1838–1897," in Hilary Beckles and Verene Shepherd, *Caribbean Freedom*, p. 323.

2. R.W. Beachy, *The British West Indies Sugar Industry in the Late 19th Century* (Oxford: Basil Blackwell, 1957), p. 120.

3. Richard A. Lobdell, "Patterns of Investment and Sources of Credit in the British West Indian Sugar Industry, 1838–1897," in Hilary Beckles and Verene Shepherd (eds.), *Caribbean Freedom*, p. 326.

4. Richard A. Lobdell, "British Officials and the West Indian Peasantry, 1842–1938," in Malcolm Cross and Gad Heuman (eds.), *Labour in the Caribbean* (London: Macmillan Caribbean, 1988), p. 199.

5. Quotations from the Report of the 1897 Royal Commission are taken from Lord Olivier, *Jamaica: The Blessed Island* (New York: Russell & Russell, 1971, first published London: Faber and Faber Ltd., 1936), p. 257.

6. Ibid., p. 258.

7. H.A. Will, "Colonial Policy and Economic Development in the British West Indies, 1895–1903," *Economic History Review*, Vol. 23 (1970), p. 136.

8. Thomas C. Holt, *The Problem of Freedom: Race, Labor and Politics in Jamaica and Britain, 1832–1938* (Kingston, Jamaica: Ian Randle Publishers), p. 335.

9. Ibid., p. 335.

10. H.A. Will, "Colonial Policy and Economic Development in the British West Indies, 1895–1903," pp. 136–137. The Cabinet, however, opposed the threat of countervailing duties. Chamberlain, in reaction, asked and received from the Treasury, £340,000 of support for the region's sugar industry, as well as negotiating the contract for a shipping line and establishing the Department of Economic Botany, later renamed the Imperial Department of Agriculture.

11. Ibid., pp. 136–137.

12. Thomas C. Holt, *The Problem of Freedom: Race, Labor and Politics in Jamaica and Britain, 1832–1938* (Kingston Jamaica: Ian Randle Publishers, 1992), p. 340.

13. West Indies Royal Commission Report, as cited in Lord Olivier, *Jamaica: The Blessed Island*, p. 255.

14. Quoted in Jay R. Mandle, "British Caribbean Economic History: An Interpretation," in Franklin W. Knight and Colin A. Palmer (eds.), *The Modern Caribbean* (Chapel Hill: The University of North Carolina Press, 1989), p. 237.

15. Woodville K. Marshall, "Peasant Development in the West Indies Since 1838," in Hilary Beckles and Verene Shepherd (eds.), *Caribbean Freedom*, p. 100.

16. Sidney W. Mintz, "From Plantations to Peasantries in the Caribbean," in Sidney W. Mintz and Sally Price (eds.), *Caribbean Contours* (Baltimore and London: The Johns Hopkins University Press, 1985), pp. 131–132.

17. Gisela Eisner, *Jamaica 1830–1930*, p. 220.

18. Woodville K. Marshall, "Peasant Development in the West Indies," in Hilary Beckles and Verene Shepherd (eds.), *Caribbean Freedom*, pp. 101–102.

19. Bridget Brereton, *A History of Modern Trinidad, 1783–1962* (Kingston and London: Heinemann, 1981), p. 94.

20. The following discussion of the Guyanese rice industry is based upon Jay R. Mandle, "Population and Economic Change: The Emergence of the Rice

Industry in Guyana, 1895–1915," in *The Journal of Economic History*, Vol. XXX, No. 4, December 1970, pp. 785–801.

21. Woodville K. Marshall, "Peasant Development in the West Indies," in Hilary Beckles and Verene Shepherd (eds.), *Caribbean Freedom*, p. 103.

22. Gisela Eisner, *Jamaica 1830–1930*, p. 289.

23. Dawn I. Marshall, "The History of Caribbean Migrations: The Case of the West Indies," *Caribbean Review*, Vol. 11, no. 1, p. 8.

24. Ibid., p. 8. Bonham C. Richardson has written two very important discussions of the impact of emigration in this period. See his *Caribbean Migrants: Environment and Human Survival on St. Kitts and Nevis* (Knoxville: The University of Tennessee Press, 1983) and *Panama Money in Barbados, 1900–1920* (Knoxville: The University of Tennessee Press, 1985).

25. Data on Guyana's death rate are taken from Jay R. Mandle, "The Decline in Mortality in British Guiana, 1911–1960," *Demography*, Vol. 7, No. 2, August 1970, Table 1, p. 303.

26. Data on Guyana's birth rate are taken from Joycelin Byrne, *Levels of Fertility in Commonwealth Caribbean 1921–1965* (Mona, Kingston, Jamaica: Institute of Social and Economic Research, University of the West Indies, 1972), Table 2, p. 48.

27. Data on death rates in Jamaica are taken from Gisela Eisner, *Jamaica 1830–1930*, Table VI, p. 137; data on the birth rate in Jamaica are taken from Joycelin Byrne, *Levels of Fertility in Commonwealth Caribbean 1921–1965*, Table 2, p. 48.

28. Dawn I. Marshall, "The History of Caribbean Migrations," pp. 8–9.

29. Ibid., p. 9.

30. Jay R. Mandle, "The Decline in Mortality in British Guiana," p. 314.

31. Arthur Lewis, "The 1930s Social Revolution," in Hilary Beckles and Verene Shepherd (eds.), *Caribbean Freedom*, p. 376.

CHAPTER 4

"Industrialization by Invitation"

Gordon K. Lewis described the unrest which racked the West Indies in the mid 1930s in the following terms. The uprisings were:

> the revolt of West Indian peasants and workers against a society in which, despite formal emancipation, they were still regarded merely as suppliers of cheap labor to sugar kings and oil barons in search of quick profits. Slavery had been abolished; but the economic foundation of slavery, especially in the general picture of land ownership had remained basically untouched.[1]

The unrest was rooted in the fact that nothing resembling modern economic growth had been experienced in the region. The West Indies still primarily relied on agricultural exports, though by this time petroleum had become economically important in Trinidad. When, during the 1930s, economic depression was experienced in the developed capitalist world, the economic decline was transmitted to the region in the form of falling prices and declining demand for West Indies exports. Further, the depression resulted in many of the migrants from the West Indies becoming unemployed and choosing to return home. These returnees from Cuba, Costa Rica and Panama themselves became a source of unrest since, as Dawn Marshall writes, they

> had become accustomed to the high wages and higher standards of living of these receiving countries.[2]

The Colonial Office, in observing the breakdown of social stability in the West Indies, came to the conclusion that a change in policy toward the region was required.[3] Up until this time official policy had been that the level of social services present in any individual colony should be no more than the colony itself could financially support. Now the view was that the West Indies required a "long-term policy of reconstruction" which would involve a growth in the supply of social services, assistance to export agriculture and a diversification of the economy, all to be financed by the Colonial Government.

The problem was that the constituency supportive of such a claim on the Exchequer was very small. As a result, there was a need to prepare and build public support for this policy change. Howard Johnson writes, in this regard, that "A Royal Commission was deliberately chosen by the Colonial Office to indicate to Parliament and the British electorate the importance of West Indian problems." The idea was that an independent and prestigious commission of inquiry could educate British public opinion concerning the need to provide financial assistance. Thus, the Commission's wide terms of reference represented an invitation for the Commission "to recapitulate, for the benefit of the British public, the social and economic conditions existing in the colonies."[4] With this end in mind, the Secretary of State for the Colonies, Malcolm MacDonald, selected the members of the West Indies Royal Commission. Chaired by Lord Moyne, who prior to becoming a Lord, was Walter Guiness a long time Conservative member of Parliament, the Commission included a broad representation of interests. Only one major constituency was omitted, as noted by Howard Johnson, and that was a member from the West Indies. Johnson argues that the reason for this omission was to placate "the prejudices of the colonial population who were more likely to accept the recommendations of a commission comprised of men of status in British society rather than one including local representatives."[5]

The Moyne Commission held hearings and carried out investigations in the West Indies from September 1938 to June 1939, finishing its report in December 1939. When completed, the Commission's report was exhaustive in its portrayal of life in the region. Gordon K. Lewis writes that "the strength of the Moyne Report ... was the remarkable candour of its examination of West Indian society."[6] Further, the Commission acknowledged that at root the social and economic problems of the region were those of underdevelopment. What the West Indies needed above all was "a substantial and steady increase in the volume of economic activity."[7] The problem was that Moyne did not lay out a strategy to achieve that goal. Again quoting Lewis, "the weakness of the Report ... was the general timidity of its recommendations."[8]

The Commission did not envision the possibility that the region's economy might experience the kind of structural transformation associated with modern economic growth. It did not foresee the possibility that the manufacturing and service sectors could grow relative to agriculture in the way which is characteristic of the modernization experience. Instead the Commission wrote, "the majority of the population must continue to depend, for a long period, if not indefinitely on export agriculture." This was because "West Indian manufacturing industries must necessarily be small and weak." Prospects for the peasantry were not thought to be encouraging and the Commission explicitly ruled out an extensive program of land settlement. It recommended that each of the West Indian governments "should have easily applied power to enable them to acquire compulsorily agricultural land which it is needed for such purpose as land settlement," but noted that such schemes "are expensive and throw a charge on the finances of the Colonies concerned that is heavy in relation to the number of persons settled."[9] Thus, despite its enlightened attitude towards social policy, the Moyne Commission did not differ from a long line of colonial policy makers. It simply did not believe that the people of the West Indies were capable of initiating a process of economic modernization. What the region needed, but the Moyne Commission did not provide, was a strategy to deal with its long-term failure to develop while simultaneously addressing the emerging problems of unemployment and underemployment. Central here, once again, was the role of the plantation sector. Though it continued to possess a concentrated control of the best agricultural land, its employment-generating capacity had been reduced. The question which should have but did not arise was whether the estates should continue to dominate the region's agricultural sector.

The Moyne Commission's failure to embrace industrialization did not occur because of ignorance of this option. Its advocacy was a principle theme in a paper submitted to the Commission by a young St. Lucian-born postgraduate student. In his memorandum, W. Arthur Lewis, the future Nobel Prize-winning economist, reviewed the desperate plight in which the West Indies found itself. His judgment was that the "gloomy prospects for agriculture the world over" required that the Caribbean look to industrialization. Lewis may not literally have been the first person to suggest this route for the region, but his 1938 position was intellectually path-breaking. He even provided a list of possible products such as refined sugar, chocolate, copra and dairy products as the kinds of industries which "the Commission would do well to consider."[10] Though there is no evidence that the commission seriously did so, Lewis' memorandum is the obvious precursor of the work he did after the war in promoting the region's industrialization effort.

Though the Commission did not advocate a change in the structure of the region's economy, it did call for the establishment of a new organization to administer assistance to the colonies in the West Indies. The Commission argued that "there is a pressing need for large expenditures on social services and development which not even the least poor of the West Indian colonies can hope to undertake from their own resources." As a result, it recommended the establishment of a West Indian Welfare Fund financed by an annual grant of £1 million for twenty years. The annual grant was to be administered by a special organization headed by a comptroller. The Commission defined the object of the fund as follows: "to finance schemes for the general improvement of education, health services, housing and slum clearance, the creation of labor departments and land settlement, apart from the cost of purchase of land."[11]

On the basis of the Moyne Commission's recommendations the British Government passed the Colonial Development and Welfare Act in 1940. Although the act did not establish a separate West Indian fund, it did provide money for schemes for welfare and development in the entire empire to come from a common source. A special organization, independent of the local governments, was created to coordinate expenditures. While no fixed annual amount was earmarked expressly for the West Indies, a Colonial Office White Paper issued in February 1940 stated that the aid to be granted to the region would approximate the amount recommended by the royal commission. Sir Frank Stockdale was appointed the first Comptroller for Colonial Development and Welfare (CD&W)in the West Indies on September 1, 1940 and by early 1941 he was in the West Indies assembling a staff for his new department.[12]

In the absence of a strategy for economic transformation, it was all but inevitable that CD&W would fail to resolve the region's long-standing inability to initiate the process of economic modernization. In Gordon K. Lewis' words CD&W "was an outfit, altogether, with a marked consumption rather than production bias, so that its schemes had little, if anything, to do with the major task of net capital improvement." In fact CD&W spent £29 million in the years through 1956 on a wide array of largely rural projects. A list provided by Lewis offers a flavor of the kinds of activities engaged in: agronomical demonstrations in Barbados, books for an Antigua grammar school, the training of nurses in Grenada, cotton variety trials in St. Vincent, a new jetty in Barbuda.[13] These were, again quoting Lewis, "piecemeal improvements of social services and agriculture rather than an attempted re-orientation of economic life."[14]

Though government policy did little to change the structure of production, World War II resulted in a movement in that direction. Particularly Trinidad and Tobago and Guyana were the beneficiaries of heightened economic activity as a result of the construction of United States military bases. Construction employment was ample and as a result unemployment decreased markedly. In addition, the fact that the region was substantially cut off from international trade meant that it had to become very largely self-sufficient at least in agricultural foodstuffs. As a result, throughout the area Government-supported "Grow More Food" programs were initiated. In these efforts plantations were encouraged to diversify their output and produce for the local market. In addition, assistance was provided to the region's farmers to increase their output of food crops.

The "Grow More Food" programs have not received the study which they deserve. Though a war-time expedient, they represented the first systematic effort to diversify the structure of the region's economy. As such they stood as a dramatic departure from the norm of export agriculture concentrated in one or a few crops which had long been characteristic of the region's economy. Seen in that perspective "Grow More Food" may well provide insights into the potential available to the region in shifting to a more diversified structure of agricultural production.

In Guyana, for example, producers of rice and ground provisions were assisted by Government.[15] Additional market depots were provided while the Department of Agriculture guaranteed prices for foodstuffs and supplied technical information. Eight District Food Committees were established in order to distribute aid for small drainage and irrigation schemes, planting material and general purpose loans. Even so, a shortage of ground provisions developed by early 1944 at which time the Department of Agriculture increased its effort to stimulate output by purchasing lorries and operating them as mobile depots. The sugar estates too were required to participate in the growing of these local foodstuffs. At first they grew root crops, but later specialized in peas and beans. The Director of Agriculture considered this diversification "perhaps Sugar's most outstanding contribution to the food problem." Overall the program could claim an outstanding success, at least with regard to output levels. The production of ground provisions was 50 percent higher in 1941–45 than it had been in 1936–40. By the end of the war plantain and cassavas were in abundance and were being exported for the first time.[16]

Though this experience was widely duplicated throughout the region, at no time was it considered to be more than a wartime expedient, to be dismantled as soon as circumstances permitted. When in Guyana "Grow More Food" was drawn to a close in 1947, the Governor argued that it had been only a "short-term policy to meet an emergency which obliged us to grow more food at any cost." He maintained that such a program could not be adopted during peace time. He pointed out that the expenses incurred by the government had been considerable, especially with regard to the financial losses sustained by the expanded system of market depots. While, he conceded, it was true that diversification of agriculture had occurred to some extent, the country was to return to less expensive agricultural policies.[17]

Though "Grow More Food" demonstrated the potential for agricultural diversification in the region, it was far from an effort at agricultural transformation. Under it, the structure of land ownership had not been altered. The plantations continued to control a very high percentage of the farm land in the region. "Grow More Food" had demonstrated the ability of the West Indies to feed itself. As such it was a refreshing illustration of productive flexibility in a region which for centuries had been wed to a single crop. It nonetheless was the case that sugar plantations still dominated agriculture.

The economic growth process would have been considerably advanced if, in the years that were to follow, the gains represented by "Grow More Food" had been built upon. This is because agriculture had and has a potentially important role to play in the process of economic modernization. Rising agricultural incomes can provide a market for a fledgling manufacturing sector either for consumer goods or agricultural implements. Such a domestic market to which local businesses could devote their initial efforts was (and is) critical to regional development. Obviously the small size of the Caribbean's population, not to say that of any one of the territories, means that domestic markets will be small in any case. Ultimately industrialization in the West Indies requires that it become successful at exporting its output. But the ability to produce export quality goods at competitive prices requires business expertise. Such competence develops as a result of coping, initially on a small scale, with both failures as well as successes in the marketplace. A local market is a necessary training ground for businesses that must advance to world markets. However, the low incomes associated with plantation agriculture limited the extent to which that training ground was provided.

In addition to creating a domestic market, a thriving agricultural sector facilitates economic development in at least three other ways. Rising incomes in the countryside may result in an increase in the level of savings generated in the region, thereby facilitating capital investment. Second, expanded agricultural output in supplying locally consumed foodstuffs in increasing amounts, can free foreign exchange which might otherwise be used for food imports. In this way growth in agriculture can facilitate expansion of other economic sectors by, for example, increasing the region's capacity to import capital equipment. Lastly, and perhaps most importantly, agriculture can be the incubus for the nurturing of the entrepreneurial and business skills associated with economic rationality and productive efficiency. As Alister McIntyre has written, the object of policy should be "to create a new generation of farmers on economic units. Businessmen not peasants."[18] The thought here is that if business competence is nurtured among West Indian farmers, then either they or their offspring will be better endowed with the human capital essential to long-term growth. In the absence of a dynamic agricultural sector the stock of such skills and attitudes may be insufficient to modernize the economy.

Because of its failure to address the land question, the Moyne Commission left in place a principal basis of the region's underdevelopment. This omission meant that nothing like the kind of reorganization of agriculture called for by McIntyre could have occurred in the years immediately after World War II. Table 1 illustrates the lopsided distribution of land which persisted in this period. The data are taken from the censuses of 1961, but the pattern which they depict is not much different than what prevailed fifteen or so years earlier. The concentration of land ownership remained profound even at this late date. Only in Trinidad and Tobago did moderate size farms cultivate more than 50 percent of acreage. Everywhere else the pattern was the same: small units represented a very high percentage of farms in cultivation, but controlled a tiny percentage of acreage under crops. At the same time, relatively few farms controlled a vastly disproportionate share of cultivated land. The most extreme case in this regard was Barbados where less than 1 percent of the farms controlled 83.1 percent of the land. Similar patterns were present in Antigua and Barbuda, and St. Kitts/Nevis/Anguilla. The pattern was only slightly less concentrated in St. Vincent and the Grenadines, St. Lucia, and Grenada where about 1 percent of the farms cultivated about half of the land in production. A somewhat more complex pattern was present in Jamaica where there was substantial land concentration, but at the same time the small and middle size farm sector was not negligible. In combination the latter controlled in excess of half the land in use. Overall, however, the pattern is clear. Despite "Grow More Food" and the decline in the overwhelming dominance of plantation agriculture in the West Indies social structure, the ownership of land still, in 1961, reflected the region's history of plantation dominance. When World War II ended, therefore, the familiar pattern of production reasserted itself. The very large number of small farms produced primarily food crops for domestic consumption, and the large estates continued to produce an export staple.

In the aftermath of World War II, the West Indian economy found itself in a frustrating cul de sac. The population and labor force were growing and rising unemployment was imminent. Living conditions therefore were at risk. The redeployment of land necessary to introduce a new dynamism into agriculture had not occurred. The Moyne Commission had not supported industrialization and yet had acknowledged the need to establish new sectors of economic activity. Thus a policy vacuum had been created which urgently

Table 1

Percentage Distribution of Farms and Farmland Acreage by Size (1961)

Country	Under 5 acres		5–50 acres		50 acres and above	
	% farms	% acres	% farms	% acres	% farms	% acres
Antigua	91.1	26.9	8.1	11.8	0.8	61.3
Barbados	98.2	13.4	0.9	3.5	0.8	83.1
Dominica	75.2	13.2	22.9	26.6	1.9	60.2
Grenada	89.6	23.9	9.5	25.3	0.9	50.8
Guyana	NA	NA	NA	NA	NA	NA
Jamaica	78.6	14.9	21.2	40.2	0.2	44.9
St. Kitts-Nevis-Anguilla	94.5	15.0	4.4	7.7	1.2	77.3
St. Lucia	80.0	15.0	19.0	33.0	1.0	53.0
St. Vincent	89.0	29.0	10.6	30.6	0.4	40.4
Trinidad and Tobago	46.5	6.9	53.2	61.8	0.3	31.3

Source: Antigua, Barbados, Dominica, Grenada, St. Kitts-Nevis-Anguilla, St. Lucia, St. Vincent: Carleen O'Loughlin, *Economic and Political Change in the Leeward and Windward Islands* (New Haven and London: Yale University Press, 1968), Table 15, p. 103; Jamaica and Trinidad: George L. Beckford, "Caribbean Rural Economy," in George L. Beckford (ed.), *Caribbean Economy* (Mona, Jamaica: Institute of Social and Economic Research, 1975), Table 1.3, p. 87.

needed to be filled both in the name of employment creation and economic development.

In this vacuum emerged the strategy of industrialization associated regionally with the name of W. Arthur Lewis. Lewis published in 1950 an article entitled, "The Industrialization of the British West Indies." Originally appearing in the *Caribbean Economic Review*, and issued in several subsequent pamphlet editions, it had became a focal point of discussion.[19] Lewis' paper built upon the memorandum he had earlier submitted to the Moyne Commission which had argued for the need for industrialization. In this version, Lewis was much more specific concerning the means by which the region could undergo a major reorientation of economic activity.

Lewis' strategy for the West Indies was informed by the theoretical approach which shortly he would publish under the title of "economic development with unlimited supplies of labor." In this model, a society experiences economic development to the extent that a modern capitalist sector drains resources from a traditional sector and grows relative to that sector. In Lewis' formal model the traditional sector is assumed to be composed of workers whose net contribution to output is either zero or close to zero. The modern sector can then entice labor to it by setting a wage rate somewhat higher than the customary income provided in the traditional sector. It will be successful in this because the traditional sector will be in no position to compete for labor services, in light of the fact that, at the margin, labor contributes nothing to production. Economic growth in this perspective is a process whereby a more productive sector grows at the expense of the less productive. Lewis does not attempt to explain the origins of the modern sector. He leaves the impression that its existence cannot be explained by the history of the country and is not something which could emerge from a dynamic which is already present in an economy. Rather it is an intervention whose interaction with the rest of the economy drains the existing sectors of their resources in the name of the growth which it alone can provide.

In accord with this model, industrialization in the West Indies for Lewis could only occur as a result of external initiatives. Foreign capitalists would have to create the modern sector by investing in the region. Indeed, foreign business investment was seen by Lewis as the sine qua non of West Indian industrial development. In his discussion of the initial sources of the entrepreneurship essential for manufacturing he considered only private foreign investors and local government. The local private sector was not taken into account.

Lewis' view was that "the islands cannot be industrialized to anything like the extent that is necessary without a considerable inflow of foreign capital and capitalists and a period of wooing and fawning upon such people." There were two arguments behind this assertion. First was the fact that industrialization was expensive, "quite beyond the resources of the islands." The second was based on the view that export promoting was too difficult for the business persons of the region. It required breaking into foreign markets and building up new distribution outlets. These would most likely be accomplished if "the islands concentrate on inviting manufacturers who are already well established in foreign markets." Only after foreign businesses had been attracted to the Caribbean would, in Lewis' scheme, a role appear for the local private sector. With the rise in output produced by foreign investors, domestic income would increase. Then, "if local people are thrifty, they can build up savings which in due course enable them, having learnt the tricks of the trade, to set up in the business themselves." In the strategy then, foreign businesses, in addition to promoting exports, had a tutorial role to fulfill. For, it is when "the local people have learnt the job and have built up their own savings that they can go right in." Thus it seems clear that the phrase coined by Lloyd Best, "industrialization by invitation," really does not do violence to the Lewis strategy.[20]

There has been a tendency to exaggerate Lewis' share of responsibility for the weaknesses of the program that ensued. In fact two of the critical features of his industrialization scheme never were realized in practice. Lewis, in the first instance, insisted that manufacturing promotion in the region could function effectively only in the context of regional integration. His words on the subject were explicit: "it is idle to talk about a serious effort at industrialization until the whole area is brought within a single customs union." Such a union was not established in the West Indies until 1974. The second major departure from Lewis' plan concerned the question of exports. Lewis had made it quite clear that the program would not accomplish its employment goals unless it successfully penetrated export markets. Lewis estimated that, of the 120,000 manufacturing jobs needed during the 1950s, production for the region's market would provide employment for only about 20,000. He thus concluded that manufacturing could not have the impact required "unless the islands start to export manufactures to outside destinations."[21] This injunction to export, however was in practice disregarded. The region's manufacturing sector did not achieve a significant export orientation. Indeed, early industrial promotion legislation was biased to import substituting rather than to exports. With such a bias the program could hardly attain the goals Lewis had set for it.[22]

In light of these shortcomings it might be argued that it is unfair to attribute the industrialization program's failure to Lewis. After all, critical elements of his strategy were never implemented. Nonetheless there is validity to the view that the region's approach to industrialization was fundamentally flawed and that its flaws were rooted in the industrialization strategy Lewis promoted. For it was Lewis who most forcefully advanced the view that foreign investment could be relied upon to achieve regional industrialization. The corollary of this emphasis on foreign investment was that the region's agriculture did not warrant priority attention. Neither of these propositions is validated by the experience of the countries which have successfully experienced growth in the twentieth century. Countries such as South Korea and Taiwan have experienced growth more dependent upon an internal dynamic than Lewis believed possible. Agricultural modernization preceded industrialization in those countries and in so doing provided the market and savings which contributed to the success of the industrialization effort. Similarly, indigenous businesses played critical roles in the industrial sector, though, to be sure, foreign investment played an important gap-filling role. It is true that the West Indies' governments, in implementing industrial promotion schemes, were not faithful to important elements of Lewis' approach. Nevertheless in a more fundamental sense they did adopt an approach which in its pessimism concerning the possibility of indigenous development was very much in the spirit of both Lewis' theory of development and specific policy recommendations.

Under the circumstances there should be no surprise to learn that, through its first two decades, the industrial promotion effort largely failed to accomplish its goal of creating enough jobs to absorb the region's growing labor force. The approach was excessively optimistic concerning the volume of investment which would come to the region and the job-creating potential of the investment which did. In the absence of the nurturing of a West Indian business sector, all the region could do was hope that overseas business people would flock to the West Indies. In the end this hope was not fulfilled.

In the first place, the little foreign investment that did come to the region was largely confined to Jamaica and to Trinidad and Tobago. Not even Barbados was the recipient of much capital inflow for manufacturing in these early years, not to mention the negligible amount which went to Guyana and the Windward and Leeward Islands. But, in the second place, even in Jamaica and Trinidad and Tobago, the effect of the investment that did arrive from abroad did not approach the hopes that Lewis had held out. There were too few projects and the projects that were undertaken were too capital intensive to prevent unemployment from rising in a context of rapid population and labor force growth. At the same time, because the projects undertaken tended to be branch-plant assembly activities, few linkages were established between them and the rest of the host economy. As a result of the latter shortcoming, indirect job creation was far smaller than anticipated.

Data from Trinidad and Tobago and Jamaica illustrate the point. By June 1963 in Trinidad and Tobago 99 factories employing a mere 4,666 workers had been put in place under that country's Pioneer Industries program. Adding to that number the 40 factories under construction and anticipating an additional 2,255 jobs that would be created, Edwin Carrington wrote in 1967 that "the estimate of 6,921 jobs from these 139 establishments and an investment of $257.8 million (TT) is to say the least disappointing." It was all the more so in view of the fact that between 1950 and 1963 Trinidad and Tobago's labor force increased by nearly 100,000 and employment in the country's sugar industry declined by about 3,800.[23] A similar pattern of inadequate employment creation occurred in Jamaica. There, while the labor force was growing by about 25,000 per year between 1956 and 1968 and the sugar industry was eliminating a total of 10,000 employment opportunities, the industrialization program created altogether about 13,000 jobs. Owen Jefferson concluded for Jamaica in tones that echoed Carrington's summary for Trinidad and Tobago: "even though there has been a relatively rapid rate of increase of production, employment has not kept pace, with a resulting tendency towards an increase in the rate of unemployment."[24] The sad fact is that the roughly 20,000 jobs created in the 1950s and 1960s through the industrial development programs were just about the same number that Lewis cited as being inadequate for the 1950s alone. Industrialization by invitation, in short, did not come close to the employment goals that had been its raison d'etre.

Despite the failure of industrial promotion to absorb the region's rapidly growing labor force, the pressures generated by that growth were somewhat offset by three unforeseen developments. First, the region experienced an expansion of the raw materials extraction sectors in the largest territories. In turn, this expansion, by augmenting government tax revenues, permitted an increase in public sector employment. During the 1950s and 1960s bauxite in Jamaica and Guyana and petroleum in Trinidad and Tobago increased output substantially. Foreign-owned, these sectors stood as enclaves in their respective surroundings. They engaged in little processing, established few linkages with other sectors of the economy, and employed relatively few workers. They did, however, contribute to government revenues through taxation. With these revenues government itself became a substantial employer of labor in these years. In this way governments came to occupy the employer role which the manufacturing sector had failed to do. In Trinidad and Tobago, for example, the roughly 82,000 workers who in 1984 were employed either as civil servants or working for state owned corporations constituted 17 percent of the labor force and 20 percent of the job holders in that year.[25] Public sector employment in Jamaica in 1976 was on the same order of magnitude. Carl Stone reports that in that year the state sector was responsible for 15.7 percent of the jobs present in the Jamaican economy.[26] No comparable data are available for Guyana, but it is almost certain that there too the government share in employment was quite high.

A second development was the emergence of tourism in the late 1950s and 1960s as a major economic activity in the region. Technological change, particularly the advent of jet air travel, resulted in a vast expansion of the market for Caribbean vacations. In response the governments in the West Indies promoted the industry through incentive legislation. Thus in Barbados, the Hotel Aid Act of 1956 promised extensive fiscal concessions for the construction of tourist accommodations, and a Barbados Tourist Development Board was established in 1958. A similar pattern was followed in Jamaica and somewhat later in the smaller islands of the Eastern Caribbean. Only Guyana and Trinidad failed to participate in the emergence of this industry. The former lacked the necessary environmental attractions while the latter seems to have eschewed the industry as a matter of preference.

Unfortunately for those who did pursue it, tourism was soon discovered to be a poor alternative to manufacturing. According to Delisle Worrell, tourism was the least labor intensive sector in the entire Barbados economy. At the same time, wages in this sector were below those of all other sectors of the economy except public administration and agriculture. In 1975 Dawn Marshall estimated that only 3,628 jobs existed in the Barbados tourist industry, employing only about 3 percent of the labor force.[27] Thus this industry only to a very limited extent filled the gap left by the failure of manufacturing.

Finally and most importantly, the region exported people, if not commodities, on a massive scale. Richardson reports that estimates of total Caribbean migration to Britain between 1951 and 1961 range between 230,000 and 280,000 with only Trinidad and Tobago failing to contribute to the outflow during these years.[28] If this estimate of the emigration is accurate and assuming that emigration from Trinidad was nonexistent, the magnitude of the migration is truly staggering. For it means that in this ten year period something on the order of 10 percent of the population of the West Indies, excepting Trinidad and Tobago, left their home to take up residence in the colonial power. It is during these years that emigration became perceived "as an integral part of the economic and social life of the British West Indian Islands."[29]

Migration to Great Britain, though, was curtailed with the passage in April 1962 of the Commonwealth Immigrants Act. In 1965, however, the Immigration and Nationality Act opened the United States to West Indian emigres. As a result, the outflow from the region continued, only with a change in destination. Table 2 reveals that starting in 1967 emigration to the United States from Barbados, Jamaica and Trinidad and Tobago (the only countries in the region for which separate data are available) abruptly increased. At their peaks emigration rates from these countries were quite high: 8.6 per 1000 in Barbados and 9.4 per 1000 in Jamaica in 1968 and 7.9 per 1000 in Trinidad and Tobago in 1970. Between 1967 and 1973 more than 150,000 persons left these three countries for the United States. Estimates prepared by Robert Harootyan and Aaron Segal suggest that emigration from the West Indies between 1950 and 1972 may have reached between 600,000 and

Table 2

Migration to the United States from Barbados, Jamaica and Trinidad and Tobago, 1963–73

Year	Barbados	Jamaica	Trinidad and Tobago	Total
1963	376	1880	448	2704
1964	393	1762	413	2568
1965	406	1837	485	2728
1966	520	2743	756	4019
1967	1037	10483	2160	13680
1968	2024	17470	5266	24760
1968	1957	16947	6835	25739
1970	1774	15033	7350	24157
1971	1731	14571	7130	23432
1972	1620	13427	6615	21662
1973	1448	9963	7035	18446

Source: Calculated from Virginia R. Dominguez, *From Neighbor to Stranger: The Dilemma of Caribbean Peoples in the United States*, Antilles Research Program, Yale University, Occasional Paper 5 (1975), Table 3, p. 72.

750,000 a number which represents perhaps 15–20 percent of the region's population.[30]

Such a massive movement could not have helped but reduce the pressure of unemployment, as it substantially decreased the region's labor force growth. It thereby removed some of the pressures associated with the failed effort at industrialization. But at the same time, such an emigration has associated with it costs as well as benefits. This is particularly the case in light of the fact that many of the West Indies emigres were professionals and skilled workers. As Jack Harewood wrote at the time, these are the kinds of workers "whom the developing Caribbean countries could ill afford to lose."[31]

The significance of the selectivity of migration will further be discussed in Chapter 5. Suffice it for now simply to note that the increased emigration to the United States was a continuation of a long-term adaptive strategy on the part of the West Indian people. As we have seen, emigration in search of employment had been undertaken throughout the nineteenth century, particularly during the depression associated with beet sugar. That migration had represented not only a means to achieve enhanced individual well-being. It also had macro-economic consequences. The early migration, in allowing the region's workers to secure non-estate work had contributed to the undermining of the plantation economy's hegemony. The post–World War II migration, however, was different. Not only was the scale of the population movement far greater than anything which had preceded it. But in addition, those who moved from the West Indies did so on a far more long-term basis than had occurred earlier. In this way permanent communities of West Indian people started to form outside of the geographic Caribbean. Thus it is that if conceived of as a nation, the people of the West Indies began to constitute a nation without borders. Geographically, the society which the region's people had created extended into Great Britain and North America.

NOTES

1. Gordon K. Lewis, *The Growth of the Modern West Indies* (New York: Monthly Review Press, 1968) p. 88.
2. Dawn I. Marshall, "The History of Caribbean Migrations," p. 9.
3. The following two paragraphs are based on Howard Johnson, "The Political Uses of Commissions of Enquiry (1): The Imperial-Colonial West Indies Context, The Forster and Moyne Commissions," *Social and Economic Studies*, Vol. 27, no. 3 (September 1978), pp. 266–272.
4. Ibid., p. 273.
5. Ibid., p. 273.
6. Gordon K. Lewis, *The Growth of the Modern West Indies*, p. 90.
7. West India Royal Commission, *Report*, Cmd. 6607 (London: HMSO, 1945), p. 247.
8. Gordon K. Lewis, *The Growth of the Modern West Indies*, p. 91.
9. West India Royal Commission, *Report*, pp. 247, 252, 278.
10. W. Arthur Lewis, "Memorandum on Social Welfare in the British West Indies," Serial no. 45 in *West Indian Royal Commission Evidence* (London: HMSO, 1947).
11. West India Royal Commission, *Recommendations*, Cmd. 6174 (London, HMSO, 1940), p. 9.
12. Sir Frank Stockdale, *Development and Welfare in the West Indies, 1940–42* (London: HMSO, 1943), pp. 1–3.
13. Gordon K. Lewis, *The Growth of the Modern West Indies*, p. 92.

14. Ibid., p. 92.

15. The following discussion is based on Jay R. Mandle, *The Plantation Economy: Population and Economic Growth in Guyana, 1838–1960* (Philadelphia: Temple University Press, 1973), pp. 114–115.

16. British Guiana, *Legislative Council Papers*, 11/1945, "Report of the Director of Agriculture for 1944," p. 2.

17. Jay R. Mandle, *The Plantation Economy*, p. 119.

18. Alister McIntyre, "Adjustments of Caribbean Economies to Changing International Economic Relations," in Lloyd B. Rankine (ed.), *Proceedings of the Sixteenth West Indies Agricultural Economic Conference* (St. Augustine, Trinidad: Department of Agricultural Economics and Farm Management, University of the West Indies, 1983), p. 19.

19. W. Arthur Lewis, "The Industrialization of the British West Indies," *Caribbean Economic Review*, Vol. 2 (1950), pp. 1–39.

20. Ibid., pp. 38–39. In a 1976 lecture at McGill University, Best claimed authorship of the phrase. See Lloyd Best, "The Choice of Technology Appropriate to the Caribbean Countries," p. 2.

21. W. Arthur Lewis, "The Industrialization of the British West Indies" pp. 30, 11, 15, 16.

22. Terrence Farrell, "Arthur Lewis and the Case for Caribbean Industrialization," *Social and Economic Studies*, Vol. 29 (December 1980), pp. 54–55, 59.

23. Edwin Carrington, "Industrialization in Trinidad and Tobago since 1950," *New World Quarterly* 4 (Crop Time, 1968), pp. 37–43.

24. Owen Jefferson, "Is the Jamaican Economy Developing?" *New World Quarterly*, 5 (Cropover 1972), pp. 1–12.

25. Trevor Farrell, "The Caribbean State and its Role in Economic Management," in Stanley Lalta and Marie Freckleton (eds.), *Caribbean Economic Development: The First Generation* (Kingston, Jamaica: Ian Randle Publishers, 1993), p. 203.

26. Carl Stone and Stanislaw Wellisz, "Jamaica," in Ronald Findlay and Stanislaw Wellisz (eds.), *Five Small Open Economies* (Published for the World Bank, New York: Oxford University Press, 1993), pp. 188–189.

27. Delisle Worrell, "An Economic Survey of Barbados 1946–1980," p. 37; Winston Cox, "The Manufacturing Sector in the Economy of Barbados," p. 65; and Edsil Phillips, "The Development of the Tourist Industry in Barbados, 1946–1980," p. 124, all in Delisle Worrell (ed.), *The Economy of Barbados, 1946–1980* (Bridgetown, Barbados: Central Bank of Barbados, 1982).

28. Bonham C. Richardson, "Caribbean Migrations, 1838–1985," in Franklin W. Knight and Colin A. Palmer (eds.), *The Modern Caribbean*, p. 216; G.W. Roberts, "Prospects for Population Growth in the West Indies," *Social and Economic Studies*, Vol. 11, no. 4 (1962), Appendix, p. 350.

29. Virginia R. Dominguez, *From Neighbor to Stranger: The Dilemma of Caribbean Peoples in the United States*, Antilles Research Program, Yale University, Occasional Paper, 5 (1975), p. 14.

30. Robert Harootyan and Aaron Segal, "Appendix: Tables on Caribbean Emigration," in Aaron Lee Segal, *Population Policies in the Caribbean* (Lexington, MA: Lexington Books, 1979) p. 219.

31. Jack Harewood, "West Indian People," in George L. Beckford (ed.), *Caribbean Economy: Dependence and Backwardness* (Mona, Jamaica: Institute of Social and Economic Research, University of the West Indies, 1975), p. 123.

CHAPTER 5

Persistent Underdevelopment

The years after World War II saw the development of a nationalist politics in the region. According to Franklin W. Knight and Colin A. Palmer the efforts of two distinct groups provided the preliminary political work essential for the successful drive to political independence. The first identified with the left of the British political system, particularly the Fabian Society. The second was, according to Knight, "a mixture of populists, independent intellectuals and those inspired by a semimillennial spiritual return to Africa."[1] The beneficiaries of these efforts were the politicians associated with the achieving of independence in the region. Included in this latter group were Norman Manley in Jamaica, Robert Bradshaw in St. Kitts and Nevis, Vere Bird in Antigua and Barbuda, Eric Gairy in Grenada, Grantley Adams in Barbados, Eric Williams in Trinidad and Tobago, and Cheddi Jagan and Forbes Burnham in Guyana.

The first fruit of the region's nationalist politics was the West Indies Federation which was inaugurated in 1958. When the Federation collapsed in 1962 the larger territories of the region — Jamaica, Trinidad and Tobago, Barbados, and Guyana — all rapidly moved to separate sovereignty. With only a short delay, the smaller territories followed suite, starting with Grenada in 1974. The process of political decolonization was completed in 1983 when St. Kitts and Nevis achieved formal political independence.[2] Subject only to the constraints imposed by size and limited wealth, the English-speaking Caribbean had become a grouping of nations whose prospects for future success lay in the efficacy of the development policies they undertook.

Table 1

1970 Gross Domestic Product Per Capita
at Factor Cost in US Dollars

Country	per capita GDP ($)
Barbados	616.8
Guyana	334.4
Jamaica	649.5
Trinidad and Tobago	859.5
Antigua	386.7
Dominica	272.5
Grenada	329.4
St. Kitts	338.5
St. Lucia	334.0
St. Vincent	215.3

Source: Calculated from Sidney E. Chernick, *The Common-
wealth Caribbean: The Integration Experience* (Baltimore:
The Johns Hopkins University Press, 1978), Tables SA2.2–
SA2.12, pp. 284–294.

By the 1970s, when the process of political decolonization was well
underway, enough economic growth had occurred in the West Indies so that
all of the territories with the exception of St. Vincent earned per capita
incomes in excess of $US 250 (Table 1). That figure represented the thresh-
old level which according to the World Bank in those years separated the
Low Income from the Middle Income countries. The plantation economy and
its aftermath while limiting economic modernization, had nonetheless allowed the West Indies to move to a higher level than the poorest of the poor
nations of the world.

Guyana, Jamaica, and Trinidad and Tobago benefitted from the mining of
bauxite and petroleum and Barbados and Antigua had already started to
increase their income as a result of the performance of their tourist industries.
But the strategy to achieve economic expansion through industrialization
had not borne much fruit. In the small Leeward and Windward Islands,

Table 2

Sectoral Contribution to GDP 1970[7] (Percent)

Country	Agriculture	Manufacturing	Mining	Services	Government
Barbados	13.9	10.8[1]	–	15.4	14.7
Guyana	19.3	12.2[2]	20.4	7.3[3]	13.2
Jamaica	7.9	13.2	15.9	11.2[4]	10.2
Trinidad and Tobago	5.2	11.7	17.7	5.9[4]	12.0
Antigua	18.8	10.2	–	16.2[5]	19.3
Dominica	26.4	8.1	–	6.3[6]	21.6
Grenada	23.7	3.8	–	2.9[5]	19.2
St Kitts	29.7	2.7	–	3.0[5]	19.8
St Lucia	22.0	3.6	–	3.3[5]	17.9
St Vincent	25.0	3.8	–	3.5[5]	20.2

[1]Manufacturing and mining. [2]Includes sugar milling and rice milling. [3]Financial services only. [4]Miscellaneous services. [5]Hotels. [6]Services and professions. [7]Omitted: construction, transportation and public utilities, distribution, renting and ownership of houses.

Source: See Table 1.

industrialization was all but absent. As revealed in Table 2, in 1970 manufacturing represented less than 10 percent of output in each of the smaller islands except Antigua, where the percentage stood at 10.2. Even in the larger nations of Barbados, Guyana, Jamaica, and Trinidad and Tobago manufacturing remained a relatively small contributor to output, standing at less than 15 percent in all cases. To place this statistic in perspective, it should be noted that the World Bank reported that as early as 1960 manufacturing in the middle income countries — the group to which the Caribbean belonged — contributed 23 percent, a percentage which increased to 32 percent by 1976.[3]

The establishment of manufacturing had been far less extensive than what would have been necessary to employ the growth in the region's labor force. In the mid-1960s unemployment in all territories where the data were made available reached double digit levels. Guyana in 1965 recorded an unem-

Table 3

Manufactured Exports as Percent of Total Exports and as Percent of Manufactured Output, 1970

	Manufactured exports as % of total exports	Manufactured exports as % of manufactured output
Dominica	10.5	9.7
Grenada	0.9	4.4
St. Lucia	NA	NA
Antigua	1.5	1.0
St. Kitts	14.3	34.6
St. Vincent	1.4	1.8
Barbados	25.6	14.9
Guyana	1.8	2.5
Jamaica	3.9	2.9
Trinidad	6.1	5.5

Source: Sidney E. Chernick, *The Commonwealth Caribbean: The Integration Experience* (Baltimore: The Johns Hopkins University Press, 1978), Table SA10.2, p. 488.

ployment rate of 20.9 percent, Barbados and Trinidad and Tobago reported 13 and 14 percent, respectively, and Jamaica in 1967 experienced an unemployment rate of 18 percent.[4] In 1970 Jack Harewood estimated unemployment in the region as a whole at between 15 and 25 percent. In addition, he estimated that in Trinidad and Tobago, the only country for which data allowed such an estimate, underemployment came to 37 percent.[5]

It is quite likely that in this period the incidence of poverty in the region actually increased. Writing at the time, Harewood noted that:

the greatest poverty is to be found in those households where there is no one capable of being in the labor force or else in households where adults of working age ... eke out an existence by employing themselves in petty jobs and self-employment of a kind that brings only the barest minimum.[6]

Between 1946 and 1960 labor force participation rates declined in every territory examined.[7] This, in combination with the rising unemployment rate, suggests the likelihood that the percentage of poverty-stricken households may have increased. At the very least it can be said that the success achieved in industrialization in this period did not substantially improve the living standards of a large proportion of the region's population.

The problem with the manufacturing sector was twofold. In the first place, it emerged as an import-substituting sector. That is, its output was almost entirely directed to the local market. As Table 3 indicates only a very small fraction of West Indian manufacturing was exported. As a result, the limited size of the regional market acted as a serious constraint to this sector's growth. In addition, the manufacturing sector which did emerge depended heavily on imported inputs. A 1978 mission from the World Bank reported that in the manufacturing sector "local value added is small, and few linkages ... have been generated within the domestic economy."[8] At least in part this dependence on imported inputs was a result of governmental policy which allowed for duty-free importing of intermediate inputs.[9] Given both the small size of the West Indian population and the fact incentives were not present to encourage manufacturing to establish extensive linkages in the local economy, this newly emerging sector could not possibly expand sufficiently to make a dent in the region's growing problem of unemployment.[10]

In failing to encourage manufacturing exports the Caribbean ignored the lessons articulated in the mid-1960s by one of its leading economists, William Demas. In a series of lectures, Demas had emphasized that in small economies such as those of the Caribbean, "the character of growth cannot be as autonomous and as self-sustaining as in a large closed economy." Structural openness, argued Demas, was the consequence of the limits size imposes both with respect to potential demand and supply. Small size means that there is little diversity in the availability of resources, a limitation which tends to narrow the range of feasible output. With diversity in production constrained, countries like those in the Caribbean are forced to specialize in production. What cannot be produced at home must be bought from abroad, and that requires export earnings. That in turn, means that they must export in order to satisfy the desires of local consumers. At the same time, small markets prevent local producers from capturing the production efficiencies associated with large-scale operations. To achieve such efficiencies and thereby maximize the incomes which can be generated from the use of modern technology, production must be oriented to export markets. Then, production will not be limited by the size of demand.[11]

Dissatisfaction with the pattern of industrial development experienced in the Caribbean was most vividly expressed by Lloyd Best. He scornfully referred to the post–World War II economy as merely a "plantation economy further modified." In this way, Best, a Caribbean nationalist, criticized the fact that the region's economy had remained "as it has always been, passively responsive to metropolitan demand and metropolitan investment." The growth experienced had not occurred in "residentiary" sectors: those which were locally owned and using an indigenously developed technology. Manufacturing, tourism, the extraction of bauxite and even the continued export of agricultural staples all involved "dependence on imported enterprise."[12]

Aside from its limited employment creating role, "industrialization by invitation" did little to enhance local technical competencies. Lewis had hoped that foreign firms would share the "tricks of the trade" with the local population. But there was nothing in that strategy which encouraged such a process of teaching and in practice it was rarely done. Alternatively, such competencies could have been developed if extensive linkages had been forged between manufacturers and local suppliers. Efficient production techniques could have been learned by local business people in supplying the inputs required by manufacturing firms. But since a domestic intermediate goods market did not appear, local firms were denied the opportunity to learn. Precisely because modern economic growth relies on technological progressivity, these missed opportunities within manufacturing were very costly. The growing gap between the managerial and technical skills present in the region and the competencies required by modern industry meant that the more the region's economy grew, the more it required expatriate entrepreneurship.

Studies undertaken at the University of the West Indies and the University of Guyana in this period illustrate the problem. In the bauxite and petroleum industries Norman Girvan reported "an extreme degree of technological dependence ... [since] the functions basic to a technological capability, such as those related to modification, initiation and innovation, are to all intents and purposes entirely absent." Even where such industries were nationalized, as in the case of bauxite in Guyana and a section of Trinidad and Tobago's petroleum industry, "technological dependence remains high," though Girvan detected "evidence of plans and arrangements for the establishment of a local technological capability, however embryonic." In tourism too, such dependency was extensive and growing. In this industry modern technology was typified by the design and equipping of hotels and the services provided. In general, Girvan reported, "technological dependence in this sector has also been on the rise." Evidence of this was that the resort style hotels introduced into the region by foreign hotel chains had increased their share of local industry, "at the expense of the small hotels and guest house segment of the industry using more traditional 'local technology.'" Finally, the same pattern of technological dependency was present in the manufacturing sector. Girvan wrote that plant technology was fundamental to manufacturing. The problem was that "the Caribbean has developed virtually no capabilities in the design, modification or even procurement of industrial plant." Necessarily, therefore, the crucial decisions made with regard to production or investment in this sector had to be taken externally.[13]

Obviously this limited technical competency was a fundamental impediment to Caribbean development. The often-repeated answer to the question of why this incapacity was present in the region blames its educational system. The argument is that the schools in the West Indies excessively emphasize the skills associated with white collar and clerical employment and insufficiently provide students with the opportunity to absorb technical skills. Thus the Annual Report of the Commissioner of Education in Guyana as early as 1925 complained that "in education beyond the primary stage there is a great lack of facilities for technical education of every kind." The Commissioner went on "there is hardly any calling — agricultural, industrial or commercial — of which even the rudiments can be satisfactorily learnt in the colony."[14] Several years later a report on educational reform for the region as a whole argued for a new type of secondary school which would be "directed essentially to the stimulation of interest in the pupils' social and industrial environment, and calculated to create a taste and aptitude for industrial, agricultural and commercial pursuits, or for social service in primary schools and elsewhere, rather than for the 'learned' professions and sedentary or clerical posts in Government service."[15] More recently, the same theme was struck by Sidney E. Chernick in a World Bank Report. Chernick argued that though "literacy rates are high, education has stressed the liberal arts along British lines." He goes on, that "technical education is gaining some ground but, by and large, the work force lacks industrial skills and attitudes."[16]

But to say that the literary content of the educational curriculum was excessive when compared to the technical component is not to respond to the question of why, in the post-independence period, a change in this orientation did not occur. With independence, the countries of the Caribbean could have initiated a process by which their students would have been exposed to a curriculum better suited to the modern world of technology than was the system inherited from the British. But such a change did not occur. Thus writing as late as 1993, a World Bank study of education in the region reported that the need for vocational training "has been stressed in virtually every major document relating to educational development in the English-speaking Caribbean in this century."[17] The failure of such educational reform suggests that there is a need to explore why strong pressures were not generated to change the content of education in the region.

The lack of inter-industry linkages is one obvious reason that there was not present a strong incentive to augment the level of technical competence present in the region. As structured, the region's economy simply did not need engineering and technological competencies in substantial numbers. The small size of the region's economy may have precluded the development of a capital goods sector. But size alone did not prevent the development of firms capable of performing maintenance, repair and modification of existing equipment. The fact that such a sector in the economy emerged only minimally represented a twofold weakness. Because of its absence not only was the region unable significantly to modify tools and machinery to make them more suited to local conditions. In addition this industrial void meant that there was very little pressure from the business community to alter the schools' curriculum to increase the supply of technically trained personnel. Thus the West Indies were caught in a negative circularity: the absence of an equipment modifying and repair sector meant that there was little demand for technical skills. But the fact that relatively few people with technical skills were present meant that the region's economy lacked the industries essential to advance its productivity.

The fact that the West Indies' agricultural sector stagnated in this period is at least one reason this circularity of underdevelopment persisted. It has long been known that in the process of modern economic growth the relative importance of agriculture declines. Nonetheless this sector's contribution to growth can be substantial. As discussed in Chapter 4, agricultural modernization facilitates economic development by augmenting savings, increasing market size, earning and/or saving foreign exchange and expanding input and output markets.

The latter contribution is particularly germane with regard to the issue of the technical skills present in the West Indies. A dynamic food producing sector could become an important consumer of the services of an equipment repair and modification sector. As agriculture became increasingly productive the region's farmers would both have the need for the services of such a sector and be able to pay for the maintenance and modifications they require. Indeed, given the structure of the West Indies economy, such a pattern of demand would be most likely to appear in agriculture. Tourism is an unlikely market since its linkages with a sector based on technical skills are confined to construction. In the manufacturing sector, the transnational firms which dominate tend to provide their own maintenance and modifications services. It is therefore only among the region's agricultural producers that local businesses concerned with design and adjustment of equipment would be

Table 4

Agriculture's Contribution to Gross Domestic Product, 1961/65–1979/81 (Percent)

Country	1961/65	1979/81
Antigua	15.5	6.9
Barbados	26.8	8.9
Dominica	37.3	36.3
Grenada	36.7	31.9[1]
Guyana	26.1	22.6
Jamaica	12.3	7.9
St. Kitts	41.0	18.5[2]
St. Lucia	34.0	14.5
St. Vincent	35.0	15.5
Trinidad	9.7	2.7

[1]1979. [2]1978.

Source: Calculated from United Nations, Economic Commission for Latin America, Office for the Caribbean, *Agricultural Statistics — Caribbean Countries* (CECAL/CARIB 82/13) Volumes IV and V (1982) Tables 4.1, p. 20; 4.3, p. 22; 4.6, p. 25; 4.8, p. 27; 4.9, p. 28; 4.11, p. 30; 4.13, p. 32; 4.14, p. 33; 4.15, p. 34; 4.17, p. 36.

able to find a market. As a result agriculture occupies a critical position in the region's efforts at economic modernization. This strategic position is occupied not so much because of the West Indies' ability to become self-sufficient in food stuffs. Rather the contribution will be made if agriculture becomes the consumer of locally designed and produced inputs. That equipment would help to raise levels of agricultural productivity. At the same time, the demand for such production would increase the need for technically trained personnel, thereby helping to move the region towards the kind of technical competence required by modern economic growth.

Unfortunately as indicated in Table 4, agriculture was not a growth sector between 1960 and 1980 in the regional economy. Its percentage contribution to gross domestic product experienced a precipitous decline between the

Table 5

Tons of Agricultural Production, 1970/74–1980/84

	1970–74	1980–84	% change
Sugar	1,240,000	830,094	–33.1
Bananas	349,869	219,336	–37.3
Citrus	219,800	94,318	–57.1
Cocoa	12,359	6,954	–43.7
Rice	142,300	184,678	+29.8
Poultry	44,000	78,020	+77.3
Beef	20,000	19,720	–1.4
Milk	99,000	83,800	–15.4
Eggs	13,507	13,880	+2.8
Fish	49,500	46,226	–6.6
Sweet potatoes	28,906	35,460	+22.7
Yams	124,394	146,537	+17.8
Cassava	53,800	27,021	–49.8

Source: Caribbean Community Secretariat, *Caribbean Development to the Year 2000: Challenges, Prospects and Policies* (Georgetown, Guyana: Caribbean Community Secretariat, 1988), Table VII.3.

early 1960s and the early 1980s. These declines, it should be noted, did not occur in economies experiencing rapid economic growth and structural transformation.Furthermore they occurred at a time when both bananas and sugar experienced favorable price movements and gross revenue in the region from these products actually increased. Their decline was entirely due to the falling trend in production. Indeed, all four of the West Indies' major agricultural exports substantially declined in production in these years. In sugar, still the most important export crop in the region, the fall in production was by about one-third, a decline which was accompanied by a decrease in output per acre of more than 10 percent.[18] Only St. Kitts and Nevis was able to experience upward movements in these measures. But dramatic downturns occurred in all of the other major producing countries: Guyana, Barbados, Jamaica, and Trinidad and Tobago. The pattern was similar in bananas. In all of the major producing territories banana production fell, most dramatically so in the country where the industry was largest, Jamaica. More rice, poultry and ground provisions were produced in 1980/84 than had been the case in 1970/74, but beef, milk, egg and fish production either fell or stagnated.[19] In any case, the scale of production of these crops, however, was insufficient to offset the downward trends experienced in the major export staples.

Thus it is that agriculture's failure meant that pressures for an enhancement of the technical skills present in the region failed to materialize. Only a limited demand for indigenously produced tools and equipment emerged in the food production sector. That, in turn, meant that the demand for the personnel necessary to produce such output similarly was constrained. As a result, the educational system experienced little or no pressure to transform itself in order to satisfy a changing pattern of demand in the labor market. Labor in the Caribbean continued to lack the expertise required by the process of economic modernization.

Not only was there minimal pressure to increase the supply of highly trained personnel domestically. It also seems clear that the emigration experienced in this period contributed to this lack of technical competence. For as revealed in Table 6 it appears that the exodus from the region disproportionately was of highly skilled individuals. As mentioned in Chapter 4, data on this subject are available only for Jamaica, Barbados, and Trinidad and Tobago. There does not appear to be any reason, however, to doubt that the experience of these countries was typical of the region. In each case professional and technical workers and managers in 1970 represented a substantially higher proportion of the workers leaving the West Indies than their share of the labor force. This most dramatically was the case in Jamaica where Professional and Technical workers constituted 6.5 percent of the labor force, but composed 13.1 percent of the emigrating workers. But what was true for Jamaican professionals was true for professionals and managers elsewhere. Everywhere these relatively skilled members of the labor force left the region in numbers greater than their proportionate share.

An examination of the occupational structure of the West Indian labor force in the United States, as contrasted to the occupations reported by migrants at the time of their relocation from the Caribbean, provides additional insight into this question. Table 7 provides information on three variables: the occupations emigrants reported in 1967, the occupational structure of West Indians in the United States in 1973, and in order to gain perspective, we in addition provide information on the occupational structure of the black labor force in the United States in that same year. As such it

Table 6

Professional and Technical Workers and Managers as Percent of Labor Force and Percent of Emigrating Workers, Jamaica, Barbados, and Trinidad and Tobago, 1970

Country	Labor force		Emigrants	
	Prof. and Tech.	Managers	Prof. and Tech.	Managers
Jamaica	6.5	0.7	13.1	3.6
Trinidad and Tobago	9.7	1.2	14.6	2.4
Barbados	9.2	1.4	14.7	1.8

Sources: Labor Force: Sidney E. Chernick, *The Commonwealth Caribbean: The Integration Experience* (Baltimore: The Johns Hopkins University Press, 1978), Table SA1.28a. p. 261; Emigrants: Calculated from Virginia R. Dominguez, *From Neighbor to Stranger: The Dilemma of Caribbean Peoples in the United States* (New Haven: Yale University, 1975), Tables 8, 9 and 10, pp. 77–79.

allows us to judge the appropriateness of the skills migrants possessed for effective participation in an economically developed country.

It is obvious that immigrants made a considerable adjustment in their occupations once having become participants in the United States labor market. Substantial continuity prevailed for professionals, technicians and managers: about one-fifth of those who left the region were employed in that category and that proportion remained about the same in the United States. But more than two-fifths of the migrants reported themselves to be private household workers when they left the region. However, in the United States less than one in twenty secured such employment. Rather what seems to have happened is that many of the people who saw themselves as household workers wound up securing employment as sales and service workers. In each case, an important occupational shift occurred, almost certainly in response to the pattern of demand for labor present in the United States. As a result of these adjustments, the West Indian labor force in the United States was employed proportionately more in white collar occupations than was the

Table 7

Percentage Distribution of West Indians Upon Emigration, 1967, West Indians in the United States, 1973 and Afro-American Labor Force, 1974 by Occupation

Occupations	West Indians upon emigration	West Indians in U.S.	U.S. Afro-Americans
Professionals, technicians, and managers	20.2	19.3	14.5
Clerical	9.1	2.8	2.3
Sales	1.2	29.3	15.2
Crafts	6.9	9.7	9.4
Operatives	8.4	13.0	21.9
Private Household	46.2	3.4	5.1
Service	6.6	19.9	20.0
Laborers	1.4	2.6	11.6
Total	100.0	100.0	100.0

Sources: Immigrants and West Indians in U.S.: Computed from Virginia R. Dominguez, *From Neighbor to Stranger: The Dilemma of Caribbean Peoples in the United States* (New Haven: Antilles Research Program, Yale University, 1975), Tables 8, 9, 10, pp. 77–79, and Table 38, p. 108–109; Afro-Americans in U.S.: Computed from Bureau of Labor Statistics, *Handbook of Labor Statistics 1975*, Table 19, p. 72.

African-American labor force. Conversely U.S. Blacks were more heavily concentrated in the relatively low skilled laborers and operatives categories.

What all of this seems to suggest is that those who left the Caribbean in these years were people capable of providing the kind of skills and possessing the adaptive ability required of a labor force in a modern or modernizing economy. On one hand the level of skills present permitted West Indian people to fill the white collar occupations which characteristically increase in association with the process of economic development. On the other hand, the shift that occurred between occupations reported at the time of the move from the Caribbean and those reported as members of the United States labor force suggests that this was also a population capable of responding speedily to labor market signals. The West Indian labor force in the United States was able to make the adjustment from the relative stagnation of the Caribbean to the greater dynamism present in the United States labor market.

It seems clear, then, that the huge volume of migration experienced in these years represented a substantial loss to the Caribbean. These obviously were people who could have by using their skills contributed to the development of the region. Particularly the professionals, managers and technicians could have made a impact on regional growth. They possessed the level of skills in scarce supply in the region. But the attractiveness of the United States labor market meant that instead of their contributing to the growth of the Caribbean, they helped augment the human capital present in the metropolitan country. The region was thus caught in a vicious cycle of underdevelopment. Given the West Indies' proximity to the labor market of the United States, the relatively low cost of air fare, and the long-established culture of migration present in the region, the relocation of people possessing the human capital associated with economic well-being reached very large proportions. Writing in the mid-1980s Aaron Segal reported that "Caribbean net migration since 1959 constitutes approximately 29 percent of all voluntary international migration — legal and illegal ... the absolute size and relative proportions of Caribbean emigration place it ahead of all other sending regions including North Africa, the Mediterranean, India, the Philippines and China."[20] As a result, the very fact of underdevelopment became the cause of continued underdevelopment. Modernization requires skilled personnel and increasingly those were the very persons emigrating from the Caribbean.

The rise in unemployment and associated poverty in the Caribbean put large numbers of the population under severe and direct economic pressure. One response to that was emigration. Another was an increase in the pressure on political leaders to do something about the region's economy. However, it was soon discovered that both the emigration and the kind of growth which had been experienced meant that little could be done locally to reverse the region's dynamic of underdevelopment. The economies of the Caribbean had benefitted from the application of modern production methods to Caribbean manufacturing, raw materials extraction and tourism. But even as that was occurring the ability of the West Indian people resident in the region to initiate economic activity in those industrial spheres deteriorated. The technological gap between the requirements of modern industry and the competencies of the people who remained in the West Indies widened as human capital emigrated.

Even as economic competence was slipping abroad in this way, self-government was increasingly on the political agenda. The region, constitutionally, was moving into a new epoch. Universal suffrage elections were held throughout the region starting from the 1950s with the clear prospect of independence in the near future. The promise of self-rule and independence raised expectations that economic policy would be more responsive to the needs of the people of the region than had been the case during the long era of colonial rule. Thus as first Jamaica and Trinidad and Tobago, and then Guyana and Barbados, achieved independence in the 1960s, party politics carried the weight of both the frustration associated with poverty and also the anticipation that in the future, the region's political leadership would be responsive to the aspirations of the people for an improved standard of living. Denis Benn writes that "by the early 1960s with self government a reality, or nearly so, for the larger territories in the region, attention shifted from the issue of political decolonisation, which had been the dominant theme in regional politics during the previous two decades, to the question of economic decolonisation. In other words, to a consideration of the changes necessary to effect an alteration in the inherited colonial economic structure."[21]

The problem was that the history of plantation dominance when combined with the more recent experience of dependent growth meant that few of the emerging local leaders possessed either competence or experience in economic management. In agriculture, plantation ownership and management had, outside of Barbados, largely been in foreign hands. The local farm sector typically was composed of individual cultivators who were almost never called upon to supervise others aside from family members. At the same time the new sectors of the economy also largely excluded West Indian people from managerial and technical responsibility. As a result, the skills present among the nationalist leaders who ascended to political power tended not to be entrepreneurial. As such they had little practical experience in the managerial side of economic activity. Thus when Charles C. Moskos Jr. surveyed the region's political leadership in the 1960s, he found a preponderance of professionals, white collar workers, and trade union leaders and very few owners or managers of private businesses.[22] The typical West Indian political leader thus was only tangentially related to the region's centers of production. As a result, such individuals were poorly positioned to influence the economic decisions by which ultimately their political careers would be measured.

The unsatisfactory nature of the economic growth which had been experienced in the West Indies in the two decades after World War II thus was present at all levels of society. Preeminently, the pressure for change was generated by the poor and the unemployed. They personally experienced the failure of dependent development and reacted with both parliamentary and extra-parliamentary pressures. It was they who were the major participants in the 1970 Black Power revolt in Trinidad, and they also supplied the mass support for Michael Manley's shift to the political Left in Jamaica in 1974. But in addition, an interest in change also was present among the region's new political elite, especially where independence was achieved. Threatened from below, but incapable of exercising much leverage over foreign firms, the leaders of Jamaica, Trinidad and Tobago, Guyana, and Barbados, all countries where independence was secured in the 1960s, searched for new structures of economic activity in their own political self-defense. By the 1970s a powerful multiclass convergence of views on the necessity for a change in economic strategy had developed.

This consensus formed around an enhanced role for the public sector in the region's economy. Increasing the role of government was a reaction to the failure of "industrialization by invitation" to satisfy the economic aspirations of the Caribbean people. It is true that the strategy had, in the larger territories, succeeded in raising aggregate income levels and in creating a manufacturing sector where previously there had been none. It however had failed to provide the new governing class with adequate instruments to ease the pressures associated with widespread poverty and unemployment. The new political rulers continued to lack economic authority. The result was an effort to correct this deficiency by placing increased economic as well as political power in the hands of governmental officials.

As can be seen in Table 8, in eight of the ten West Indian territories the role of government in the economy, as measured by its percentage contribution to output, increased between the early 1960s and 1980s. In general the most dramatic increases in this measure occurred in the bigger islands, the ones which had by then experienced some degree of industrialization. Guyana's increase was the most dramatic, more than doubling. However Barbados and Jamaica each experienced an increase in the role of government of about 50 percent, and Trinidad and Tobago 39 percent. Of the smaller territories only the Windward Islands of Grenada and Dominica experienced an increase of at least 40 percent. Elsewhere among this grouping, the increases were either small, as in the case of St. Lucia and St. Kitts/Nevis or negative as occurred in Antigua and Barbuda and St. Vincent and the Grenadines. In those places, however, even after a decline was experienced, the government's role in the economy remained substantial, 15.1 percent in the case of Antigua and Barbuda and 18.7 percent for St. Vincent and the Grenadines. Thus during the late 1960s and the 1970s the response to

Table 8

Government Services Percentage Contribution to Gross Domestic Product at Current Factor Cost, 1963 and 1984

Country	1963	1984	% increase
Antigua and Barbuda	19.0	15.1	−20.5
Barbados	9.6	14.3	49.0
Dominica	16.0	23.0	43.8
Grenada	14.3	19.9[1]	39.2
Guyana	10.2	22.3	118.6
Jamaica	7.3	11.6	58.9
St. Kitts and Nevis	17.0	19.0	11.8
St. Lucia	18.1[2]	19.6	8.3
St. Vincent and the Grenadines	19.1	18.7	−2.7
Trinidad and Tobago	10.0[3]	13.9	39.0

[1]1980. [2]1964. [3]1962.

Source: Calculated from Ramesh Ramsaran, *The Commonwealth Caribbean in the World Economy* (London: Macmillan Caribbean, 1989), Table 2.5, pp. 46–47.

continued economic frustration was an enhanced role for the government in economic affairs.

Specific political and social circumstances determined the ideological defense which was mounted to justify the enhanced role for the state in the economies of the region. Three countries — Jamaica, Guyana, and Grenada — articulated explicitly socialist justifications for the new approach. In contrast, no such ideological commitment was present in Barbados, Trinidad and Tobago, or in the other countries of the Eastern Caribbean. Nevertheless the role of government grew almost everywhere. Of Barbados, John Mayers wrote in the early 1980s that, "though basically conservative and capitalist, with a history of tolerance and laissez-faire attitudes, [it] has had a proliferation of statutory bodies over the past fifteen years."[23] The growth of the public sector in Trinidad and Tobago was similarly non-ideological, though extensive. Trinidad and Tobago's government invested in a long list of directly productive economic activities including sugar, petroleum, fertilizer, iron and steel, shipping, airlines, and banking.[24] Sometimes private sector bankruptcy proceedings, and not broad strategies, forced the hand of regional governments. When the private airline which serviced the Leeward and Windward Islands collapsed, those governments took over LIAT Airlines in order to protect themselves from a potentially disastrous shutdown of regional air transportation. Similarly, the government of St. Lucia took over two hotels held by LIAT's former owners in order ensure that they remained open.[25]

But if it is true that out of self-defense West Indian ruling elites moved to increase the role of government in the regional economy, it is not necessarily the case that doing so accomplished what modern economic growth requires. The region's economy had to be made, in Demas' words, "flexible, adaptable and ready to introduce innovations, whether cost-reducing or product introducing."[26] The degree to which the new state-based strategy of economic development succeeded in moving the regional economy in that direction is the issue to which we turn in the next chapter.

NOTES

1. Franklin W. Knight and Colin A. Palmer, "The Caribbean: A Regional Overview," in Franklin W. Knight and Colin A. Palmer (eds.), *The Modern Caribbean* (Chapel Hill: The University of North Carolina Press, 1989), p. 10.

2. At present Montserrat, the British Virgin Islands, the Cayman Islands, and the Turks and Caicos Islands are Crown Colonies with limited internal self-government. Anguilla is an Associated State of Britain.

3. The World Bank, *World Development Report 1978* (Washington, DC: The World Bank, 1978), Table 3, p. 80.

4. Jack Harewood, "The Under-Utilization of Available Human Resources," in Jack Harewood (ed.), *Human Resources in the Commonwealth Caribbean* (Trinidad: Institute of Social and Economic Research, University of the West Indies, 1970), p. 5.

5. Jack Harewood, "West Indian People," in George Beckford (ed.), *Caribbean Economy*, p. 14.

6. Ibid., p. 18.

7. Carmen McFarlane, "The Employment Situation in Overpopulated Territories in the Commonwealth Caribbean," in Jack Harewood (ed.), *Human Resources in the Commonwealth Caribbean*, pp. 4–12.

8. Sidney E. Chernick, *The Commonwealth Caribbean: The Integration Experience*, Report of a Mission sent to the Commonwealth Caribbean by the World Bank (Baltimore: The Johns Hopkins University Press, 1978), p. 181.

9. Ibid., pp. 182–183.

10. Ibid., p. 181.

11. William G. Demas, *The Economics of Development in Small Countries with Special Reference to the Caribbean* (Montreal: McGill University Press, 1965), pp. 61, 74.

12. Lloyd Best and Kari Levitt, "Character of Caribbean Economy," in George L. Beckford (ed.), *Caribbean Economy*, pp. 37, 52.

13. Norman P. Girvan, *Technology Policies for Small Developing Economies: A Study of the Caribbean* (Mona, Jamaica: Institute of Social and Economic Research, University of the West Indies, 1983), pp. 48–49, 52.

14. "Major Bain Gray's Report, British Guiana, 1925," in Shirley C. Gordon (ed.), *Reports and Repercussions in West Indian Education, 1835–1933* (Aylesbury, England: Caribbean Universities Press/Ginn, 1968), p. 151.

15. "The Marriott Mayhew Report, 1933," in Shirley C. Gordon (ed.), *Reports and Repercussions in West Indian Education, 1835–1933*, p. 181.

16. Sidney E. Chernick, *The Commonwealth Caribbean: The Integration Experience* p. 201.

17. The World Bank, *Caribbean Region: Access, Quality and Efficiency in Education* (Washington, DC: The World Bank, 1993), p. 94.

18. Economic Commission for Latin America, *Agricultural Statistics — Caribbean Countries, Vols. IV and V, 1982* (Port of Spain, Trinidad: Economic Commission for Latin America, 1982), Table 11.3, p. 45.

19. For additional insight into the experience of foodcrops generally see, Lloyd B. Rankine, "Towards the Development and Design of an Appropriate Strategy to Improve Production and Productivity in the Root Crop Industry of the Commonwealth Caribbean," in David Dolly (ed.), *Rootcrops in the Caribbean*, Proceedings of the Caribbean Regional Workshop on Tropical Root Crops, Jamaica, April 10–16, 1983 (Trinidad: University of the West Indies, 1984), p. 118.

20. Aaron Segal, "The Caribbean Exodus in a Global Context: Comparative Migration Experiences," in Barry B. Levine (ed.), *The Caribbean Exodus* (New York: Praeger, 1987), p. 45.

21. Denis Benn, *The Growth and Development of Political Ideas in the Caribbean, 1774–1983*, p. 84.

22. Charles Moskos Jr., *The Sociology of Political Independence* (Cambridge: Schenkman Publishing Company, 1967), Table 4, p. 33.

23. John Mayers, "An Overview of Public Enterprises in Barbados," in *Studies in Caribbean Public Enterprise*, Volume I: *An Overview of Public Enterprise in the Commonwealth Caribbean* (Georgetown: Guyana Institute of Development Studies, and Mona, Jamaica: Institute of Social and Economic Research, 1983), p. 13.

24. Trevor M.A. Farrell, "The Caribbean State and its Role in Economic Management," in Stanley Lalta and Marie Freckleton (eds.), *Caribbean Economic Development: The First Generation*, pp. 211–214.

25. Patrick Emmanuel, "Public Enterprises in the West Indies Associated States," in *Studies in Caribbean Public Enterprise*, Vol. 1: *An Overview of Public Enterprise in the Commonwealth Caribbean* (Georgetown, Guyana: Institute of Development Studies, and Mona, Jamaica: Institute of Social and Economic Research, 1983), p. 45.

26. William G. Demas, *The Economics of Development in Small Countries*, p. 61.

CHAPTER 6

The Left Regimes

JAMAICA 1972–80

The Cabinet formed by Michael Manley upon the victory of the People's National Party (PNP) in the Jamaican election in 1972 has been described as "liberal, middle class, technocratic and sophisticated ... steeped in the social welfare traditions of activist government."[1] As such it immediately set to work to develop policies to address Jamaica's problems. The first two years of the PNP government saw initiatives in many directions. It moved to create a literacy program, a program to lease idle land to peasants, youth and adult training efforts, and a lowering of the voting age to 18. It set up a network of rural community health workers, introduced food subsidies, made secondary and university education free, and established a public works program to create jobs. In all of this the Manley Government managed not to alienate the local business community. Early in 1973 the managing director of the *Daily Gleaner*, a local newspaper which soon would become bitterly hostile, was quoted as saying "people are saying that the government's approach to social programmes is reasonable and the country has rallied nicely to the economic measures."[2]

But in March 1974 the Manley Government initiated negotiations with the bauxite companies in Jamaica to raise their taxes. The outcome of these negotiations was anything but amicable. The tension and disagreement between the Manley Government and the bauxite industry initiated a long and debilitating period of tension between the public sector and Jamaica's private sector — both foreign and local.

Output of bauxite and alumina had grown steadily in Jamaica since production was first initiated in 1952. By 1970 the four foreign-based companies involved in the industry were responsible for 41 percent of Jamaica's exports and the industry was the country's largest source of foreign exchange. Even so, the role that bauxite played in Jamaica's economy was a center of dispute. In the first place, the mining industry was a virtual enclave: neither forward nor backward linkages to the local economy had been established. Thus it was thought by members of the government that bauxite had inadequately acted as a motor for economic modernization.[3] Second, it was argued that bauxite was inadequately taxed.[4] Even relatively cautious observers agree that the rate of taxation negotiated when the industry was first established included "embarrassingly low royalty and tax rates."[5] Increases in these rates were negotiated in 1957. However the problem was more serious than merely establishing an adequate tax rate. The difficulty was in determining on what basis to tax. This issue arose since the bauxite mined in Jamaica was not in reality sold in a market where prices were competitively determined. Rather, the ore was transferred for processing by one branch of an aluminum company to another branch of the same company. A formal payment was made in such a transfer, known as a "transfer price." But since it was not a market-determined price, it could be set arbitrarily, or more likely, at a level which would minimize the overall tax liability of the firm. In Jamaica, Norman Girvan, the leading Caribbean student of the industry who later became an important figure in the Manley Government, argued that "because of the peculiar problem of taxing a commodity which is not sold, but merely transferred between branches of the same company, the industry has been considerably under-taxed."[6]

The discussions between the government and the bauxite companies over taxation were fruitless. In less than two months an impasse in negotiations was reached. When the talks broke down, the Government unilaterally moved to raise taxes on bauxite. The Government avoided the problem created by transfer prices by calculating the new tax as a percentage of the price aluminum received in the commodities market. In that way taxes would not be based on the arbitrarily set price reported by the companies, but rather would be tied to a price determined in commodity markets. The new bauxite levy was made retroactive to the beginning of 1974 and it was anticipated that the new tax would raise revenue seven-fold. Generally the tax worked as anticipated. As Ransford W. Palmer later wrote, "the Jamaica bauxite levy ... must rank as one of the finer strategies by a developing country to increase its share of the gains from commercial exploitation of its natural resources while at the same time insulating its revenues against inflation abroad."[7]

Certainly the bauxite levy resulted in a very large increase in the revenue received by the Jamaican Government. As reported in Table 1, taxes paid by the bauxite industry increased almost seven-fold in 1974 compared to 1973.

Table 1

Jamaica Government Revenues from the Bauxite Industry: Taxes and Royalties, 1964–73, Levy 1974–83 ($US million)

Year	Taxes and royalties	Year	Taxes and royalties
1964	20.52	1974	179.99
1965	22.09	1975	150.43
1966	27.53	1976	139.40
1967	24.29	1977	180.99
1968	24.33	1978	194.25
1969	29.49	1979	190.28
1970	35.95	1980	205.71
1971	30.21	1981	192.99
1972	28.42	1982	135.51
1973	26.95	1983	121.34

Source: Omar Davies, *An Analysis of Jamaica's Fiscal Budget*, Occasional Papers Series, Department of Economics, University of the West Indies (1984), p. 4.

Though there were occasional dips in the level of this public sector revenue, the end of the decade of the 1970s saw taxes paid from the industry approximate $(US) 200 million, a far cry from the roughly $(US) 25–30 million generated throughout the 1960s and early 1970s. Seen from this point of view, the levy was a success. The Prime Minister himself, Michael Manley, subsequently argued that the bauxite strategy "was a major achievement that will endure."[8]

But the success of the bauxite levy is ambiguous once attention is turned to issues other than revenue received by the Government. For, as Table 2 indicates, bauxite and alumina production declined substantially in the years after 1974. Whether this decline was a response by the bauxite corporations to the rise in the costs the levy imposed on their Jamaican operations, or whether it was, in Michael Kaufman's words, "a conscious company policy

Table 2

Bauxite and Alumina Production, Jamaica, 1972–80 (metric tons)

Year	Bauxite	Alumina
1972	12,989	2,087
1973	13,600	2,506
1974	15,328	2,874
1975	11,570	2,259
1976	10,296	1,639
1977	11,434	2,047
1978	11,736	2,141
1979	11,505	2,074
1980	12,064	2,395

Source: Carl Stone and Stanislaw Wellisz, "Jamaica," in Ronald Findlay and Stanislaw Wellisz (eds.), *Five Small Open Economies* (New York: Published for the World Bank by Oxford University Press, 1993), Table 4-30, p. 183.

to punish the Manley government"[9] for the tax is not clear. The downward trend in production is however obvious. What is also clear is that a very high level of animosity had been created between the bauxite companies and the government. In this now poisoned atmosphere any hope that the corporations would extend their range of production processes, or forge linkages with other sectors of the business community, was out of the question.

The bauxite companies' reluctance to extend operations was part of a more general pattern which appeared in the country — the unwillingness of the private sector, both domestic and foreign, to undertake investment projects. Table 3 makes it clear that while the levy allowed the public sector substantially to increase the ratio of its investment to the gross domestic product, the opposite trend occurred with regard to both foreign direct investment and investment by the local private sector. At its peak the ratio of total investment to the gross domestic product exceeded 30 percent in both 1971 and 1973. In the years thereafter and despite the fact that the rate of

Table 3

Gross Domestic Investment, Foreign Direct Investment, Public Investment and Local Private Investment, Jamaica, 1971–81 (Percent of GDP)

Year	(1)* Gross domestic investment	(2)* Foreign direct investment	(3)* Public investment	(4)* Local private investment
1971	32.1	11.2	6.7	14.3
1972	27.3	5.4	6.7	15.2
1973	31.5	3.8	6.0	21.7
1974	24.3	0.9	11.9	11.4
1975	25.8	−0.1	12.5	13.3
1976	18.2	−0.0	15.1	3.1
1977	12.2	−0.3	13.6	−1.1
1978	15.0	−1.0	17.7	−1.6
1979	19.2	−1.1	13.2	7.1
1980	15.9	1.0	17.7	−2.8
1981	20.3	−0.4	15.4	5.3

*(4) = (1) − [(2) + (3)].

Sources: Gross Domestic Investment and Foreign Direct Investment: calculated from The World Bank, *World Tables 1993* (Washington, DC: The World Bank, 1993); Public Investment: Evelyne Huber Stephens and John D. Stephens, *Democratic Socialism in Jamaica: The Political Movement and Social Transformation in Dependent Capitalism* (Princeton: Princeton University Press, 1986), Table A.2, p. 377.

public investment doubled between 1973 and 1975, overall the investment ratio fell to a low of 12.2 percent reached in 1977. Foreign direct investment had started to dry up in 1972 and continued to do so until substantial levels of disinvestment occurred at the end of the 1970s. Local investment, by contrast, held up well in the early years of the Manley Government. But the rate of local private investment fell by almost 50 percent in 1974, recovered slightly the next year, and then plunged to disastrously low levels, including disinvestment levels, in 1977 and 1978. Clearly the investment climate for private firms had turned negative and at least in part this was the legacy of the bauxite levy.

It also was the consequence of the Manley Government's promoting of "democratic socialism." Officially a political education campaign concerning democratic socialism did not occur until November 1974, though work on the concept and the Prime Minister's endorsement can be traced to the immediate aftermath of the election of 1972. The fact is however that the concept of democratic socialism was not intended to be threatening to the private sector. In identifying countries with which it shared "socialist" convictions, the Manley Government named Sweden, Holland, Britain, New Zealand, Tanzania, Australia, and India. Pointedly omitted from this list was Cuba, a country with which Jamaica had recently established diplomatic relations, China, or indeed any of the countries of the communist bloc. The democratic socialist program did not envision nationalization, expropriation or a substantial change in economic ownership. Despite the fact that Manley declared that "the days of capitalism are over.... Socialism is running the country now," he also acknowledged that "private enterprise and economic activity can be a most effective way of producing the general run of services in a country." The PNP pamphlet on democratic socialism specifically noted that private foreign capital remained welcome in Jamaica.[10]

Despite this formal ideological moderation, the 1974 democratic socialism offensive energized the Jamaican people and tended to take on a life of its own. Government-sponsored rallies were well attended throughout the country. The campaign for democratic socialism seems to have unleashed a deeply felt hope among many Jamaicans that, at last, present in the country was a government committed to egalitarian values and the dignity of the population. Michael Kaufman writes, in the aftermath of the bauxite levy and the articulation of democratic socialism by the PNC, "overall the party's popularity was higher than ever."[11]

But associated with such an ideological campaign are profound risks. Especially these risks are strong in a country as dependent on foreign investment for its economic growth as Jamaica had been. Sources of investment capital abroad possess the power to undermine that growth simply by deciding not any longer to invest in the country. Precisely such a decision becomes more likely when the adoption of a new ideology threatens to upset the stability or even the perception of the stability of the receiving country. Many variables enter into a business decision to invest. The presumption is that so long as an investment project is profitable, capitalist inflows will continue. But profits can only be anticipated; they are never certain. There is always risk associated with a decision to invest. As a result, a subjective assessment of circumstances must inevitably be part of the investment decision-making process. A socialist ideological offensive, no matter how moderate its actual content, runs the risk of creating sufficient uncertainty so that potential investors may hold back on committing to projects in a country. In that situation a "strike of capital" occurs.

This is what occurred in Jamaica. Apparently from the earliest days of the new administration, foreign investors were concerned enough to pull back on their commitments to projects in the country. Local businesses were not as skittish, with their investment levels holding up until 1974 and then only collapsing entirely in 1976. By then even public investment was in decline, partly because of declining bauxite production and partly because revenues from the bauxite levy were being used to support a severely deficit-ridden budget. Thus by 1976 if depreciation were taken into account, it is likely that investment was at so low a level that productive capacity was almost certainly in decline. Jamaica clearly was in crisis. Having adopted policies which put at risk traditional sources of investment, it had not devised an alternative to foreign dependency as a means to advance the country's productive capacity. The decline in the flow of private capital into Jamaica meant not only that the country's ability to produce was eroded. It also presented short run difficulties in satisfying two different financial needs that emerged in this period. In the past, private foreign investment provided much of the financing required to cover both Jamaica's excess of imports over exports and also the government's budgetary deficit. But during the 1970s the adequacy of this source of financing declined markedly. During these years both the trade and budget deficits tended to rise while private investment from abroad tended to fall. To the extent that the need for credit for the two deficits exceeded private investment in the country, the Government was required to borrow the balance from abroad. Thus, declining private foreign investment in the country in combination with increased credit requirements meant that the Government was forced to become a heavy debtor in overseas money markets.

Table 4 reveals the extent to which this occurred. In the years between 1972/3 and 1975/6 the Government's borrowing requirements more than tripled to almost $(J) 400 million, a level in excess of 15 percent of the country's gross domestic product. The need to borrow to finance the current account deficit grew more over these years than was the case concerning the budgetary deficit. Nonetheless the need to borrow from abroad to cover the government's revenue shortfalls increased by more than five fold during this four year period. The result was, as Compton Bourne writes, that for the government "the quantitative importance of commercial credit (essentially commercial bank loans and suppliers credit) increased" in these years.[12]

Table 4

Foreign Borrowing Requirements, Jamaica, 1972–76 [$(J) 000]

		1972–73	1973–74	1974–75	1975–76
(1)	Budgetary deficit	74.0	95.4	233.1	299.3
(2)	Domestic borrowing	53.3	64.3	112.4	192.5
(3)	Foreign borrowing for budget[1]	19.1	31.1	120.7	106.8
(4)	Current account deficit	196.7	247.6	91.9	282.8
(5)	Direct foreign investment	97.2	71.5	23.3	−1.8
(6)	Foreign borrowing for for current account[2]	99.5	176.1	68.6	284.6
(7)	Total foreign borrowing[3]	118.6	207.2	189.3	391.4

[1](3) = (1) − (2). [2](6) = (4) − (5). [3](7) = (3) + (6).

Sources: Budgetary Deficit and Foreign Borrowing for Budget: Calculated from Evelyne Huber Stephens and John D. Stephens, *Democratic Socialism in Jamaica* (Princeton: Princeton University Press, 1986), Table A.2, pp. 377–378; Current Account Deficit and Direct Foreign Investment: World Bank, *World Tables 1993* (Washington, DC: The World Bank, 1993), p. 346.

It was this growing indebtedness which marked the turning point for Michael Manley's government and democratic socialism in Jamaica. The debt crisis took the form of a scarcity of foreign exchange, a shortfall which posed a dire threat to the viability of the country's economy. This threat existed because of Jamaica's extensive reliance on imports, both in consumption and as inputs in its own production. As Kari Polanyi Levitt has put it, "without a critical minimum of foreign exchange to purchase essential imports of fuel, basic food and industrial goods, the Jamaican economy would collapse."[13] The country's mounting indebtedness, however, threatened this lifeline. If potential commercial lenders concluded that Jamaica no longer was creditworthy, they could shut off future credit in the form of foreign exchange, thereby threatening the country's ability to produce and consume.

To forestall this threat, the Government, secretly in the Fall of 1976, initiated talks with the International Monetary Fund (IMF).[14] The Government's intention was to obtain loans which might otherwise become unavailable from commercial sources. But it knew that to do so it would have to agree to the kind of conditions which the IMF everywhere imposes on borrowers. These conditions in principle are intended to reduce the degree to which a country requires credit. The IMF demands reductions in government spending in order to minimize the public sector debt and almost always advocates a currency devaluation in order to promote export sales. But such policies exact a heavy cost on the welfare of the population, particularly the poor who typically are the beneficiaries of precisely the government programs which are cut and are unable to defend themselves against the inflation which often accompanies a devaluation of the currency. Thus it was that representatives of the Manley Government approached the IMF only very reluctantly. For they knew that IMF conditions represented abandonment of the commitments for which democratic socialism had come to stand. Michael Manley, himself, in a speech in January 1977 declared that

> The Government on behalf of the people will not accept anybody anywhere in the world telling us what we are to do in our own house and in our own house there will be no other masters but ourselves. Above all, we are not for sale ... we reject any foreign imposed solution to the present crisis we face.[15]

Two weeks later Prime Minister Manley rejected a currency devaluation and conspicuously failed to engage in major reductions in government spending. Instead he announced a package of policies including an increase in taxes for individuals receiving relatively high incomes, measures to conserve foreign exchange, declared his intention to nationalize three banks, and imposed a six month freeze on prices and wages.[16] The hope was that in this way the government would be able to avoid making a formal commitment to an IMF conditionality loan.

The Prime Minister, in addition to resisting the IMF in this way, authorized the preparation of an alternative strategy of economic development to be devised by Left members of the Government and their sympathizers. This came to be known as the Emergency Production Plan (EPP). But if the Prime Minister had hoped that the Left economists to whom he entrusted the Emergency Production Plan would devise a means to resolve the country's debt crisis, he must have been bitterly disappointed. For instead of a program designed to show how the country could live within its capacity to earn foreign exchange, what emerged was a more ideological document, a plan whose goal was to "establish a true socialist order."[17] Whereas the Left could have written a plan to allocate fairly the austerity which Jamaica's indebtedness had made inevitable, the EPP instead called for a reconfiguration of the economy in which the country's banks, flour mill, cement plant and oil refinery would be nationalized, cooperative and socialist organizational forms would be supported, incentive schemes to encourage foreign investment would be dismantled, small scale and cooperative agriculture would be assigned priority attention, and the market for the country's tourism would be reoriented to deemphasize "the traditional upper middle-class Americans from the Eastern Seaboard."[18]

What the EPP failed to do in advancing its plan for socialism was to address successfully the financial problem facing the country. Thus while the government's budgetary deficit in 1975–76 was already at an unacceptably high level of about $(J) 300 million, the budget deficit included in the plan was even higher, estimated to be between $383.0 and $550.3 million.[19] The failure to solve the foreign exchange constraint was even more serious. The Plan required $350.3 million of foreign exchange, $145.3 million more than the Government estimated was available in 1977. This shortfall the Plan suggested could be made up by a combination of $35.0 million of additional aluminum sales to the socialist bloc, $58.0 million of credit from the same source, and a moratorium on the payment of private debts and investment income.[20]

There was no credibility to this strategy for overcoming the country's foreign exchange shortfall. To begin with, the EPP failed to consider how likely it was that the Soviet bloc would assist Jamaica in the way called for in the plan. Stephens and Stephens report that the Prime Minister in fact did raise the question of credit with Moscow and the OPEC countries and found no encouragement from either.[21] Even more importantly, there was absolutely no discussion of the implications of the country's imposing a moratorium on the repayment of debt and investment income. But the absence of discussion did not mean there was no problem in this regard. For, such a moratorium would have had profound implications for the ability of the country to raise financing from any source and would have immensely worsened the already difficult situation the country was facing with regard to the availability of credit. Manley, in particular, reacted negatively to the plan's unrealistic foreign exchange requirements, arguing that the plan contained "a general miscalculation about the amount of foreign exchange that would be needed and could be forthcoming."[22] The defenders of the plan argued that it was "as realistic as we could make it given the conditions under which we put it together." But Kaufman probably has it right when he argues that the "goal of the [N]ational [P]lanning [A]gency draft was not realism per se, but a realistic proposal for structural economic change."[23] The EPP was first and foremost a political document advocating a movement to socialism. Solving Jamaica's twin debt crises required a package of policies which would have involved increased taxation, reduced government spending, a program to stimulate exports and a means to limit imports. Such a package was what was necessary in order to control the country's immediate problem of mounting indebtedness while remaining faithful to the commitments of democratic socialism.

In what seems to have been a face-saving gesture, the Manley Government announced that it had adopted an Emergency Production Plan in April 1977. But it was a plan without the socialist content of the original. At about the same time the Government conceded defeat and announced that it would attempt to negotiate a loan with the IMF. Stephens and Stephens report that "the decision to go to the IMF was a defeat and bitter disappointment for the PNP left."[24] By July an agreement with the IMF had been reached in which Jamaica was to be loaned $ (US) 74.6 million over two years, a loan which was subject to IMF tests of austerity.

Though Manley argued that there was no necessary conflict between the commitment to democratic socialism and the agreement with the IMF it is clear that that was at best wishful thinking. This became all the more obvious when in December 1977 the country narrowly failed one of the IMF performance tests. In response the IMF imposed even more stringent terms on the country which effectively eliminated whatever scope remained for the Manley Government to pursue its egalitarian objectives. Government spending as a percentage of GDP was to decline from 23.7 to 20.2 percent, the budget deficit was to decrease from 13.4 to 4.5 percent, subsidies on goods and services produced by public enterprises were to be eliminated, wage increases were to be limited to 15 percent per year, while at the same time a substantial devaluation of the Jamaican dollar was to be permitted. It was, in short, a standard IMF package in exchange for which the IMF agreed to provide U.S. 240 million in loan funds during a three year period.[25] Further adjustments in the IMF agreement were negotiated during the remaining years of the PNP Administration. But by this time it was obvious that "democratic socialism" in Jamaica had come to an end.

GRENADA 1979–83

After a decade of opposition to the arbitrary rule of Prime Minister Eric Gairy, the New Jewel Movement (NJM) seized political power in Grenada in a coup which occurred on March 13, 1979. The party justified its action by asserting that it moved in this way only after having learned that the Prime Minister had issued an order to assassinate eight leading members of the party. An attack on the barracks of the country's military was successful and within in two hours political power had passed from Gairy to the People's Revolutionary Government (PRG), headed by Maurice Bishop. In a speech at 10:30 AM the new Prime Minister declared that the army had been "completely defeated and surrendered" and called "upon the working people, the youths, workers, farmers, fishermen and middle-class people and women to join our armed revolutionary forces at central positions in your communities and to give them any assistance which they call for." In that speech Bishop declared that "this revolution is for work, for food, for decent housing and health services and for a bright future for our children and great grand children." He assured "the people of Grenada that all democratic freedoms, including freedom of elections, religious and political opinion, will be fully restored to the people."[26] In short, Bishop promised both economic development and democracy and the Grenadians responded enthusiastically. As Hugh O'Shaughnesy says, "the coup was enormously popular with Grenadians and it seemed as if the whole of the island was coming out into the streets to celebrate."[27]

At the time of the Revolution, Grenada was, even by Caribbean standards, a poor nation. Its agriculture was technologically backward and dominated by the traditional export crops of nutmeg, bananas, and cocoa. Only a luxury tourist industry had emerged to complement agriculture, with manufacturing's contribution to output negligible.

Economic growth did occur in Grenada during the years of the PRG with the country's real gross domestic product increasing by about 10 percent between 1979 and 1982. Virtually all of the growth, however had its source in the construction industry and within that sector, the building of a new international airport at Pt. Salinas dominated. Other sectors, such as manufacturing and agriculture contributed only negligibly or not at all. Grenada itself was not able to finance the construction of the new airport. Thus virtually all of the growth experienced in these years was based on the government's ability to secure financing from external sources. Of the $38.7 million required for the airport's construction only $0.8 million came from domestic sources.[28] Even under the PRG, Grenada had not yet discovered an indigenous source of development.

Not only was the building of the airport a source of growth in the short-run, but the international airport was also the center piece of the PRG's economic strategy. In the 1983 budget, Deputy Prime Minister Bernard Coard wrote that its opening would represent "the beginning of a whole new economic era for our country."[29] Concerning the airport, two years earlier, Maurice Bishop had told the Grenadian people that "we must all be clear that this project represents the single most important project for our future economic development."[30]

The PRG's commitment to tourism and the airport, however, raises troubling questions. These questions have nothing to do with the American government's allegation that the airport would be used as a staging ground for regional revolution or terrorism. Rather the issue is twofold: first, whether tourism in a country like Grenada is a sector which can be seen as an agent of modernization. The issues raised here concern both the extent to which the industry raises domestic incomes and whether the skills and attitudes generated by the industry are appropriate for the process of modern economic development. The second is whether a regime like that of the PRG, given its ideological commitments and world view, can realistically promote the expansion of such a sector.

There is no doubt that there was in Grenada the potential for an expanded tourist industry and that a new airport would have helped in that process. Air service to the country was inadequate, in large measure because the existing airport lacked runway lights. No landings therefore were possible after sunset, a handicap which meant that virtually all North Americans intending to come to Grenada were required to spend a night in a neighboring Caribbean island while en route. Prime Minister Bishop gave voice to the frustrations involved when he said "coming to Grenada right now is like a labor of love. You have to be a martyr to want to come. The amount of trouble will make you sick."[31]

But for a leftist regime like that of the PRG the building of a new airport would not have ensured a successful expansion of tourism. Direct flights from the United States would have necessitated a bilateral aviation agreement between the two nations. Failing this, American tourists, the principal consumers of Grenada's product, would still be required to change flights elsewhere. But such an agreement with the United States was by no means a certainty, given the ideological hostility directed from that source to the Grenada Revolution. Indeed, a strategy of economic growth with the airport and tourism at its center would have strengthened the United States' bargaining position in its efforts to influence policy in Grenada. The threat of withholding agreement to an aviation treaty would have given the United States an important lever to influence developments on the island.

There is, in addition, a profound paradox for a leftist government like the PRG to be promoting tourism. Virtually without exception, the nationalist left in the region has taken the position that local benefits from this industry are frequently overstated and in any case not worth the cultural and political price which the creating of a "welcoming society" necessitates. Frank Taylor, for example, has argued in Jamaica's tourism "the conception of the black masses as hewers of wood and drawers of water is still very much in evidence." As such, he writes, "it perpetuates the dependency syndrome in Jamaican society."[32] V.S. Naipaul has put the issue in even more dramatic terms. Naipaul writes that "every poor country accepts tourism as an unavoidable degradation. None has gone as far as some of the West Indies islands which, in the name of tourism, are selling themselves into a new slavery."[33]

It is therefore difficult to envision the PRG successfully promoting tourism. Though its members undoubtedly shared in the conviction that the industry was degrading, they would, at the same time, have been called upon to promote it. The fact is that, as Ambursley wrote at the time, "the expansion of Grenada's tourist industry will undoubtedly result in ever greater exposure to Western lifestyles and consumption patterns" and would have tended to "undermine the regime's efforts to develop a socialist and collectivist consciousness amongst the masses."[34] The PRG would, in short, have been required to implement policies in which they simply did not believe. It is not possible to know how the PRG would have resolved this dilemma, but it is likely that, with government officials both attracted and repelled by the industry, tourist promotion might have been fitful and inconsistent. If so, it is hard to imagine that the industry could have successfully filled its role as a leading sector of economic growth.

Aside from these political and cultural concerns, on strictly economic grounds the case for tourism is not overwhelming. It is true that tourism is an industry in which the Caribbean obviously has a comparative advantage. The region's climate and access to the sea allows it to provide the services many vacationers seek. Further, since the industry caters to overseas consumers, it earns foreign exchange, enabling the region to buy from abroad much more than it would be able to do in its absence. Finally the industry both employs labor in countries with chronically high unemployment rates and pays taxes to perpetually underfinanced governments.

But these advantages can be overstated. Tourism tends to be a capital intensive, but low wage paying industry. These characteristics become all the more pronounced when the industry expands beyond the providing of luxury services and moves to a lower income segment of the market. Second the stimulation the industry provides to other sectors of the economy and to government revenue is limited by the fact that it is highly import-dependent. Much of the content of the tourist product — ranging from food to equipment — is imported, thereby limiting its local multiplier effect. The income generated by the industry disproportionately is leaked abroad, thereby failing to result in expanded sales and output locally.

The biggest problem of all, however, is that the skills associated with this industry are not those needed in a society attempting to experience economic modernization. Aside from a thin managerial level, tourism does not require a technologically sophisticated labor force. As a result its presence does not produce pressure on society's governmental and educational institutions to supply highly educated and technically skilled individuals. If tourism does not literally require hewers of wood and drawers of water, it is true that for the bulk of the industry's labor force, the skill requirements are not high. Thus the presence of this industry does not propel the society in the direction of the kind of technical competence associated with modern economic growth.

For a variety of reasons then, the PRG's view that tourism was the sector which could lead Grenada to economic modernization was probably in error. A more modest goal for the industry certainly was appropriate. Tourism can serve a valuable function in a broad strategy of growth, particularly with regard to the earning of foreign exchange. But to think that it can do more than that is both to exaggerate the likely pace of its development and to underestimate the requirements of modern economic growth.

In addition to tourism, the PRG's economic program emphasized the importance of stimulating agricultural output. In his 1983 Budget presentation, Coard declared that "agriculture is the main pillar of our economy." He went on to assert "agriculture has to develop rapidly if we are to achieve certain goals of the Revolution." Among the goals cited were a reduction in imported food, the emergence of agro-industries, the earning of foreign exchange, increasing employment and raising the living standards of farmers and agricultural workers.[35] The problem was that agriculture in the past had provided no indication that it could make the contribution that Coard called for. Agriculture's contribution to GDP during the 1976–79 period of $(EC) 32.5 million was about 11 percent lower than the level achieved during 1961/65.[36]

The structure of land holding in Grenada was a major source of the problem. Unlike a country like Barbados, the old style plantation dominance no longer was present in Grenada. What emerged in its wake was a dual agriculture sector, composed of numerous very small farms coexisting with a relative handful of large holdings, many of which were owned by the Government. Almost nine out of ten farms in the country were less than five acres, a size which was too small to permit full-time employment.[37] Furthermore, with such small holdings, the introduction of modern equipment, necessary to raise levels of agricultural productivity, was not feasible. At the other end of the spectrum, there were in 1975 ninety-nine farms of 100 or more acres.[38] These farms seem to have been cultivated at a very low level of intensity. Coard reported that when the PRG took power in 1979, one-third of the cultivatable land in the country was unused, and that "by far the greatest amount of idle land lies on the big private estates."[39] Underutilization of cultivatable acreage and low levels of productivity, in short, characterized agriculture. Agriculture in Grenada required a major reorganization if it were to make a positive contribution to economic modernization.

There has been a long history of debate in the Caribbean concerning the form such a reorganization should take. Official policy has ranged between the nationalization of estates and putting them under a centralized state management to the allocation of very small holdings to party followers and others as a form of political patronage. In contrast, the major thrust of academic work on the subject has emphasized the need to allocate land to skilled farmers in holdings large enough to accommodate modern inputs. This work takes its lead from Alister McIntyre who argued for the need to create "a new generation of farmers on economic units, businessmen, not peasants."[40] Thus L.G. Campbell notes that it is necessary to create a form which "can avoid the disadvantages of both the large plantation as well as the very small farm operations." According to Campbell the size of such units will vary according to soil and climate conditions. But the unit should be large enough, he writes, to "allow successful operation essentially by the efforts of the owner alone and perhaps some family help at peak work loads, using high technology inputs, and which is capable of yielding to the owner or operator an income no less than that earned by skilled workers in urban occupations or other business operations."[41]

Despite its recognition of the need for land reform and the extensive discussion of that subject among sympathetic scholars, the PRG during its years in power did little to change the structure of agriculture in the country. In 1982 it did pass a Land Utilization Act which allowed it to take out a compulsory lease of ten years on estates of over 100 acres on which land was idle or underutilized. But by October 1983, when it lost power, the government had not extensively employed this act. As a result throughout the reign of the PRG, Grenada's agricultural sector changed little. There remained a great many very small and fragmented farms, while a handful of large private estates and state farms, the legacy of the Gairy years, controlled between them probably half of the land in agricultural use.

This caution in approaching agriculture did not, however, reflect satisfaction on the part of the Government with the performance of this sector. Coard, in his 1983 Budget address, reiterated the urgency of raising levels of agricultural productivity. He pointed to the need to introduce new methods of production and new crops and to raise the educational level of the agricultural labor force. Coard was particularly critical of the functioning of the state farm sector. He pointed out that the Grenada Farms Corporation (GFC), the umbrella organization administering the government farms, had produced only 37 percent of its targeted output. He detailed the weaknesses of the organization and management of the corporation, complaining that the GFC had not even been able to supply his office with information essential to formulate the budget. Levels of productivity remained low: "on all of the

GFC farms primitive methods of agriculture are still being used." Overall, Coard concluded that the GFC "has not begun to fulfill the purpose for which it was created," namely, the stimulating of the agricultural sector.[42]

The problem was that though the status quo in agriculture signalled difficulties for the PRG over the long run, by 1983 it still had not adopted a strategy for change. What made this such a problem was that it was success in agriculture, not tourism, which was essential if the PRG were to move the country in the direction of economic development. Coard was right when he said that agriculture was the "foundation for anything we shall achieve in the future."[43] The PRG's airport/tourist strategy was based on the premise that linkages between tourism and the rest of the economy could be forged. What that specifically meant was that the hotels and restaurants in Grenada would be able to supply themselves with domestically grown agricultural produce. With the resulting increased agricultural production would come a rise in the income levels of Grenada's farm and rural population. But for that to be realized, an agricultural structure had to be created to accommodate and facilitate expanded output. In its absence, an enlarged tourist industry would be forced to import its food supply and as a result whatever stimulative effect tourism might potentially be responsible for would be dissipated in a flood of imports.

What seems to have immobilized the PRG with regard to agriculture was a conflict between its own ideological preferences for a dominant state sector in agriculture and the unsatisfactory performance of the GFC. In a Central Committee Resolution on Agriculture marked "Confidential" the New Jewel Movement had committed itself to the "strengthening of the State Sector" in agriculture and to beginning "the process of collectivization and transformation" of the countryside. The party's policy was to make the state-owned GFC "the leading vehicle ... for the socialist transformation of agriculture."[44] But in light of the GFC's inefficiency, there was no point in providing additional land to this public sector firm. As a result the PRG seems to have concluded that at least until such time as the state farm sector's productivity could be substantially improved it would adopt a hands off attitude towards the ownership structure of Grenada's agriculture.

A long delay in securing such gains in public sector agriculture, or a failure to do so at all, however, posed grave risks to the Grenada Revolution. For if it turned out that Grenada's state farms did not become more productive and if its small farmers were incapable of doing so, then the effectiveness of its tourist strategy of economic growth would have been blunted. The Grenada Revolution did not last long enough to judge the outcome of these difficulties. Certainly at the time of its demise the PRG had achieved very little in agriculture. If the new airport had opened in 1984 with the New Jewel

Movement still in power, the domestic food sector would not have been able to meet the growing needs of the arriving guests if indeed there were any. Food imports would have mounted, undermining the stimulus provided by tourism.

It is not possible to know with certainty how the PRG would have reacted to such a situation. It is possible that with the passage of time, the state farms would have proved themselves adequate to the task. If so, then gradually the airport/tourist strategy would have yielded positive results. But if these farms did not adequately increase their productivity, the PRG would have been required to face some difficult choices. In those circumstances the government might have had to consider an alternative which it had to date chosen to ignore: allocating land in large units to commercially successful private farmers. At once such an approach promised the modernization of agriculture, but at a cost which the PRG might have found ideologically unacceptable. Facilitating the establishment of successful commercial farmers might have been perceived by the government as creating a class which potentially represented an opposition to its socialist orientation. If this had been the case, the promotion of capitalist agriculture in this way is something which, in all likelihood, the PRG would have resisted.

The choice between capitalism and continued agricultural stagnation would have been difficult for the government. If the regime had resisted establishing technologically progressive farmers, it might have been faced with perhaps an even more unpalatable choice. For, with the construction of the airport and the expansion of tourism, agriculture's failure would have resulted in Grenada's becoming precisely the kind of welcoming society what was so much an anathema to the Revolution's leaders and its supporters throughout the region.

At it was, however, the PRG did not have to confront such a dilemma. Rather it imploded and destroyed itself. Both the regime itself, the Prime Minister and uncounted numbers of others were the casualties of a profound political crisis. In part this crisis was the consequence of mounting economic pressures, due to a slowing of foreign assistance and the ideological opposition to it by the Reagan administration in the United States. These, in turn, reinforced and contributed to increasing tensions domestically and particularly among the cadres of the ruling party. A very small number of individuals had been called upon to do the multitude of different tasks associated with the paternalistic nature of Leninist governance. The pressure from domestic and external sources finally became unbearable, giving rise to a violent fracturing of the party. With that, the Grenada Revolution came to an end.

GUYANA 1972–85

In the years immediately after independence in 1966, Guyana like other countries in the Caribbean, adopted the development strategy recommended by W. Arthur Lewis. Guyana, however, was poorly positioned to attract investment capital from abroad. The country had between 1962 and 1964 been the site of a terrifying period of conflict between its major ethnic groups — black descendants of slaves and East Indian descendants of indentured immigrants. In addition, the leading party in the colony and the leader of that party — the People's Progressive Party (PPP) and Cheddi Jagan — had been accused by the British of being communists. The interrelated divisions and tensions which resulted from this combination of communal strife and ideological polarization resulted in very little investment from abroad. The Guyana government's 1973 *Annual Economic Survey* summarized the country's difficulties quite succinctly: "despite numerous incentives and encouragement in the form of tax holidays and duty free concessions [manufacturing] remained dormant with very little expansion and diversification." Guyana's economy was dominated by the plantation cultivation of sugar, the peasant cultivation of rice, the expatriate mining of bauxite, and the production of alumina. In its first years of independence, Guyana, in short, was a nation deadlocked in its effort to achieve economic development.

Forbes Burnham and the People's National Congress (PNC) had first come to power in coalition with a small right wing party. Largely supported by Afro-Guyanese and itself nominally a socialist party, Burnham however was under much more pressure from his political left than his right. Jagan's PPP, rooted in the East Indian population, continued to be the single most important party in the country and at the leadership level routinely employed the language of Marxism–Leninism. Thus Burnham's decision to shift to the Left in the late 1960s and early 1970s made political sense. In a context in which the agenda was set from the left, more was to be gained by attempting to be more radical than Jagan and the PPP than in adopting a more centrist political stance. As a result in 1970 Burnham declared Guyana to be a Cooperative Socialist Republic. In 1972 the PNC Government nationalized the principal firm in the bauxite industry. Nationalizations followed quickly in large sections of trade, distribution, transportation, communications and the remaining firm in bauxite. Finally, in 1976 the government nationalized the economy-dominating sugar industry. By 1977, the government estimated that about 80 percent of the economy rested in the hands of the public sector.[45]

In addition to these domestic initiatives, Guyana's reputation as a radical state was further reinforced in the 1970s by its foreign policy. Long before

Table 5

Guyana Gross Domestic Product at Factor Cost
1976–90 (1977 G$ millions)

	GDP	% change		GDP	% change
1976	1050		1984	821	+2.1
1977	1019	–3.0	1985	829	+1.0
1978	990	–2.8	1986	831	+0.2
1979	976	–1.4	1987	805	–3.1
1980	992	+1.6	1988	785	–2.5
1981	989	–0.3	1989	751	–4.3
1982	886	–10.4	1990	726	–3.3
1983	804	–9.3			

Source: The World Bank, *Guyana: From Economic Recovery to Sustained Growth* (Washington, DC: The World Bank, 1993), Table 2.1, p. 119.

the other Caribbean countries followed its lead, Guyana sought out friendly relations with the Cuban government of Fidel Castro. Furthermore, it actively supported the guerilla forces of the MPLA in Angola by permitting planes carrying Cuban troops to Africa to refuel at Timehri International Airport. In both of these actions, Guyana allied itself with revolutionary forces and thus risked antagonizing the major conservative power in the region, the United States.

In both dismantling the ownership structure of the domestic economy and in its foreign policy initiatives, the Burnham government made a clean break with colonialism. Expatriate ownership of the economy was terminated, as was an unquestioning acceptance of the foreign policy positions of the advanced capitalist countries. But whatever credit can be assigned to the PNC Government for setting Guyana on an economic and diplomatic path of its own choosing was more than offset by its failure successfully to promote the economic development of the country. The Guyanese economy under the PNC simply fell apart. While Guyana in the 1960s had been considered a poor colony with a promising future, in DeLisle Worrell's words, "by 1984

Table 6

Production of Selected Products, Guyana, 1975–90 (000 Tons)

Year	Sugar	Rice	Dried bauxite	Calcined bauxite	Alumina
1975	300.0	175.8	1350.0	778.0	294.0
1976–78	299.6	167.8	956.6	669.3	258.0
1979–81	289.6	157.4	1015.2	555.0	179.4
1982–84	260.5	168.7	838.7	400.3	93.0[1]
1985–87	218.7	191.7	964.6	489.9	–
1988–90	156.5	207.8	998.0	365.3	–

[1]Production of alumina ceased in 1983.

Sources: 1976–90: Computed from The World Bank, *Guyana: From Economic Recovery to Sustained Growth* (Washington, DC: The World Bank, 1993), Table 7.1, pp. 149–150; 1975: Clive Y. Thomas, *The Poor and the Powerless: Economic Policy and Change in the Caribbean* (New York: Monthly Review Press, 1988), Table 11.6, p. 258.

the economy had been badly savaged and there seemed little hope of recovery in the near future."[46]

Tables 5 and 6 make clear the extent of the savaging to which Worrell refers. The country's gross domestic product after adjusting for price changes declined continuously in the years after 1976 (Table 5). This economic collapse was particularly devastating in the early 1980s. Between 1980 and 1984 the gross domestic product declined by almost 20 percent. After a very weak recovery another precipitous decline occurred, this time by 12.6 percent over the four year period, 1986–90. Overall the country's gross domestic product in 1990 was almost one-third lower than it had been at the beginning of the decade. By the end of the 1980s, Guyana was considered to be the poorest country in the Western Hemisphere, having beaten out Haiti for this dubious distinction.

Three productive sectors, sugar, bauxite and rice dominated output in Guyana. Production in two of them, sugar and bauxite all but collapsed during these years. Sugar production in 1988–90 stood at 156,500 tons compared to a level of about 300,000 tons which prevailed in the mid- and late 1970s. If anything, the experience was even worse in bauxite. The production of alumina, the processing stage which contributed the highest value-added to the Guyana economy, completely ended in 1983. Calcined bauxite production at the end of the period stood at a level of only 47 percent of that of 1975. Dried bauxite production fell by 26 percent during these same years. Rice, a crop grown by small farmers, did not suffer as much as sugar and bauxite. But during the mid-1980s even it was producing at a level lower than ten years earlier. Even if the growth of an underground economy means that these data may overstate the magnitude of the economic decline which was experienced in the country, overall Worrell's conclusion that "the Guyanese economic record for 1970–84 is remarkably dismal" seems correct.[47]

This economic debacle has been the subject of very little scholarly investigation. In his review of the situation, Clive Thomas is unsparing in his criticism of the PNC, but is at pains to argue that the problem was not government domination of the economy. He acknowledges that declining production occurred at the same time as the expansion of the state sector. But his assertion "that this should not be taken to mean that state control per se is necessarily inefficient, but rather that the *specific* nature of the state and political configuration in Guyana since independence has been problematic" is not convincing.[48] Thomas does not clearly delineate what it was about the Guyanese state which produced economic decline, though he is outspoken in his condemnation of use of the state to enrich PNC members and the increased bureaucratization and militarization of the society which its rule produced.

Worrell, on the other hand, convincingly argues that it was a lack of highly trained public employees which doomed Guyana's state-based development efforts. He writes that "none of the nationalization programs undertaken in the Caribbean was particularly successful and Guyana's contributed to the very serious decline in output that country experienced." Worrell argues that governments were led astray by the fact that "many leading public servants are a match for their counterparts" in the private sector. But the problem is that "the majority of the public sector is not of this caliber." As a result, when, in Guyana, the government "began by stripping the public service of leading decision-makers to staff state corporations ... there were not enough to go round."[49] The nationalizations were rushed, giving insufficient time to work out "teething problems." In addition ineffective information systems were present meaning that it was not possible effectively to monitor the public sector's performance. Worrell concludes that it is "difficult to see how Guyana's precipitate nationalization policies might have had any positive outcome."[50]

But in the context of Guyana's social structure, this dilution of managerial competence was only part of the problem. In addition, the political history of the country made it difficult for PNC managerial appointees to command the loyalty of the East Indian labor force. This was particularly the case in the sugar industry where Indo-Guyanese were numerically dominant. The PNC had been estranged from the East Indian population since its split from the then dominant PPP in 1955. After that the fundamental cleavage in Guyanese politics had been ethnic, with the PNC the party of the minority Afro-Guyanese population while the PPP became the party of the majority East Indian population. The basic demography of the country meant that the PNC could not win a fair election. Instead, in order to retain power, it resorted to electoral fraud. As a result, when the PNC took over sugar it was faced with a labor force hostile and distrustful, one which it was all but impossible to mobilize effectively and efficiently.

The sugar industry was nationalized in 1976. As indicated in Table 7, labor relations thereafter in the industry not only were tense, but over time tended to deteriorate. Days lost per employee because of strikes tended to rise throughout the decade of the 1980s, reaching a peak in 1989 when almost a full month of work per employee was lost because of labor disruptions. In the fever-charged atmosphere of Guyanese politics, and where the union which represented the sugar workers, the Guyanese Agricultural Workers Union (GAWU), was affiliated with the opposition PPP, it is hard to mistake what was going on here. The sugar industry was a sphere of Guyanese society where the Indo-Guyanese population and political structure were able to meet the government effectively in combat. The strike activity suggests that they were not bashful about exercising their leverage.

In open economies such as Guyana's, production shortfalls immediately become export declines. These, in turn, threaten to create a current account deficit in which imports exceed exports. The balance between the two must be made up. Typically this is done by borrowing from abroad in which the country receives capital inflows adequate to finance the excess of imports over exports. In the case of Guyana, however, as Table 8 indicates this did not happen. Consistently through the 1980s the overall trade balance (the current account deficit, minus the amount financed through capital inflows) remained negative and in excess of $(US) 100 million per year. That balance either was paid for by a change in the Bank of Guyana's reserves or it was not paid for at all: what is described as an increase in commercial arrears. As the table reveals, during the mid-1980s the latter is what was done. Between 1980 and 1983 accumulated arrears grew by almost $(US) 140 million. As the World Bank described it, the Government "ceased making payments to

Table 7

**Labor Days per Employee Lost Because of Strikes
in the Sugar Industry**

Year	Employees	Labor days lost	Labor days lost per employee
1980	31128	60593	1.95
1981	31374	110118	3.51
1982	30540	127987	4.19
1983	30756	164309	5.34
1984	28104	144157	5.13
1985	26700	208443	7.81
1986	24158	135109	5.59
1987	25260	128986	5.11
1988	24198	231089	9.55
1989	25502	594339	23.31
1990	30963	229291	7.41

Source: The World Bank, *Guyana: From Economic Recovery to Sustained Growth* (Washington, DC: The World Bank, 1993), Tables 1.2 and 1.3, pp. 116–117.

most of the bilateral and multilateral lenders."[51] Guyana in short approached the end of the 1980s bankrupt. Only at the end of the 1980s and under the close monitoring of the International Monetary Fund, did Guyana move away from steadily increasing indebtedness.

Thus Guyanese "cooperative socialism" was an economic disaster. Only after President Forbes Burnham's death in 1985 was the leadership of the country prepared to take stock of its situation and consider the need for a redesign of its economic strategy. But by that time, Guyana had been devastated and it obviously was going to take a long time to recover the ground which had been lost.

Table 8

Change in Components of Guyana's Balance of Payments, 1976–90 (U.S.$ millions)

	Current account	Capital account	Overall balance	Arrears	Net reserves
1976–79	−87.6	41.0	−46.6	6.9	39.8
1980–83	−151.6	29.6	−122.0	34.7	87.3
1984–87	−123.9	−28.4	−152.3	6.8	145.5
1988–90	−127.9	259.8	131.9	−29.4	−102.5

Source: The World Bank, *Guyana: From Economic Recovery to Sustained Growth* (Washington, DC: The World Bank, 1993), Table 3.1, p. 124.

CONCLUSION

The Left's experience with economic policy-making clearly was a failure. The economies of both Jamaica and Guyana deteriorated badly under Michael Manley and Forbes Burnham. Such a decline was not experienced in Grenada during Maurice Bishop's brief period of rule. Nevertheless, it is far from obvious that the PRG's commitment to tourism represented an effective strategy to promote Grenada's economic development. The Left in short had not discovered a means by which the region could escape its underdevelopment. Norman Girvan's characterization of the weaknesses of the governance by the left in Jamaica is appropriate for Guyana and Grenada as well. Girvan writes that "much of the problems encountered by the 'Democratic Socialist' project of the PNP was its failure to develop an economic strategy which was both consistent within itself and with its social and political objectives."[52]

In each case the fall of the left has been followed by more conventional economic strategies. As of this writing, however, it is too early to assess the effectiveness of these new policies in Guyana. After President Burnham's death in 1985 the country moved only hesitatingly towards economic liberalization. But with the introduction of a new Economic Recovery Program (ERP) under President Desmond Hoyte in 1988, Guyana decisively moved in the direction of welcoming foreign investment, reducing consumer subsidies, easing import restrictions and moving to privatize state holdings. These policies were continued when the PPP was elected to office in 1992. Initial indications are that these policies have provided some upward thrust to the economy. But there simply is not enough evidence available to suggest that the Guyanese economy has embarked upon a long-term path of economic modernization.

The same is true for Grenada. Tourism in the country has increased since the end of PRG rule. As a result, economic growth averaged a substantial 5.5 percent per year between 1985 and 1989. But agriculture has grown only very slowly in these years, standing in 1991 at a level only 3.8 percent higher than it had in 1984. In the meantime, the government has come to regret its decision in 1986 to abolish the country's income tax and instead rely exclusively on a value added tax. In the words of a World Bank report "public finances have consistently weakened in recent years and the public sector is facing a fiscal crisis." The public sector deficit combined with the country's current account deficit came to 52 percent of GDP in 1991. The debt service on the required loans was beyond Grenada's ability to pay and as a result it accumulated external arrears equal to 13 percent of GDP.[53] Obviously Grenada still has a long way to go before it can be said that the foundation of a modern economy is in place.

Jamaica's experience in the aftermath of left economic policy is the most extensive of the three nations. Even after the PNP's removal from office in 1980 and the accession to office of the conservative Jamaica Labor Party (JLP) under Edward Seaga, the country's relationship with the IMF remained mutually unsatisfactory. Consistently through this period the country failed the performance tests of austerity imposed by the IMF. The result of these failures was the need to renegotiate the terms upon which Jamaica was provided with financial support. Between 1981 and 1988 Jamaica entered into five different IMF agreements and agreed to three World Bank Structural Adjustment Loans. In the mid-1980s the terms associated with these loans became more stringent, until finally there was a relaxation in 1987. There seems to have been a recognition by the lenders that what they were demanding with regard to fiscal policy, trade liberalization, and the rest of their policy prescription was simply beyond the country's capacity.[54]

The expressed intention of the policies emanating from the official multilateral lending agencies is to increase the availability of investment funds and the rate of investment. In so doing, it is reasoned, the country's productive capacity will be enhanced. Clearly this has not happened in Jamaica. Table 9 reports on the country's investment rate during the entire twenty year period since the early 1970s. While it is true that the investment rate in the most recent period, 1986–90 is slightly higher than it had been during the

Table 9

Gross Domestic Product at Market Prices and Gross Domestic Investment, Jamaica, 1971/75–1986/90 (millions of 1987 Jamaica dollars)

	(1) Gross domestic product	(2) Gross domestic investment	(3) Investment as % of GDP
1971–75	18351	7541	44.1
1976–80	16256	3943	24.2
1981–85	15635	3770	24.1
1986–90	16912	4384	25.9

Source: The World Bank, *World Tables, 1993*, pp. 344–345.

Manley years, 1976–80, it obvious that it has not returned to the level reached in the early 1970s.[55] Similarly while since 1985 the country's gross domestic product has increased, it is nonetheless the case that this measure during 1986–90 stood below the level reached in 1971–75. The policies associated with the international banking community have, in short, only marginally been more successful than those associated with the left. Certainly as in the case of Guyana and Grenada there is no compelling evidence to suggest that the return to economic orthodoxy has put Jamaica on the path of modern economic growth.

NOTES

1. The Epica Task Force, *Jamaica: Caribbean Challenge* (Washington, DC: Epica Task Force, 1978), p. 314.

2. Michael Kaufman, *Jamaica Under Manley: Dilemmas of Socialism and Democracy* (Westport CT: Lawrence Hill & Co., 1985). p. 76.

3. Norman Girvan, *Foreign Capital and Economic Underdevelopment in Jamaica* (Jamaica: Institute of Social and Economic Research, 1971), pp. 41–61.

4. Ibid., pp. 61–71.

5. DeLisle Worrell, *Small Island Economies: Structure and Performance in the English-Speaking Caribbean Since 1970* ((New York: Praeger, 1987), p. 111.

6. Norman Girvan, *Foreign Capital and Economic Underdevelopment in Jamaica*, p. 261.

7. Ransford W. Palmer, *Caribbean Dependence on the United States Economy* (New York: Praeger Publishers, 1979), p. 118.

8. Michael Kaufman, *Jamaica Under Manley*, p. 85.

9. Ibid., p. 106.

10. The Epica Task Force, *Jamaica: Caribbean Challenge*, p. 68, and People's National Party, *Democratic Socialism for Jamaica*, Kingston [1974?], p. 3.

11. Michael Kaufman, *Jamaica Under Manley*, p. 93.

12. Compton Bourne, "Government Foreign Borrowing and Economic Growth: The Jamaican Experience," *Studies in Rural Finance*, Agricultural Finance Program (The Ohio State University, May 28, 1980), p. 8.

13. Kari Polanyi Levitt, *The Origins and Consequences of Jamaica's Debt Crisis, 1970–1990* (Mona, Jamaica: Consortium Graduate School of Social Sciences, 1991), p. 2.

14. Evelyne Huber Stephens and John D. Stephens, *Democratic Socialism in Jamaica: The Political Movement and Social Transformation in Dependent Capitalism* (Princeton: Princeton University Press, 1986), pp. 148–149.

15. Quoted in Evelyne Huber Stephens and John D. Stephens, *Democratic Socialism in Jamaica*, p. 150.

16. Michael Kaufman, *Jamaica Under Manley*, p. 133.

17. The EPP was subsequently published as George Beckford, Norman Girvan, Louis Lindsay and Michael Witter, *Pathways to Progress: The People's Plan for Socialist Transformation, Jamaica 1977–78* (Morant Bay, Jamaica: Maroon Publishing House, 1985), p. 21.

18. Ibid., pp. 36–38, 47, 88.

19. Ibid., p. 107.

20. Ibid., pp. 107–109.

21. Evelyne Huber Stephens and John D. Stephens, *Democratic Socialism in Jamaica*, p. 167.

22. Michael Manley, *Jamaica: Struggle in the Periphery* (Oxford: World Media Ltd., 1982), pp. 154–155.

23. Michael Kaufman, *Jamaica Under Manley*, p. 139.

24. Evelyne Huber Stephens and John Stephens, *Democratic Socialism in Jamaica*, p. 178.

25. Compton Bourne, "Jamaica and the International Monetary Fund: Economics of the 1978 Stabilization Program," *Studies in Rural Finance*, Agricultural

Finance Program (Columbus: The Ohio State University, May 29, 1980), pp. 20–21.

26. Prime Minister Maurice Bishop's first address to the nation is reproduced in D. Sinclair DaBreo, *The Grenada Revolution* (Castries, St. Lucia: A MAPS Publication, 1979), pp. 348–350.

27. Hugh O'Shaughnessy, *Grenada: Revolution, Invasion and Aftermath* (London: Sphere Books Limited, 1984), p. 79.

28. Bernard Coard, *Report on the National Economy for 1981 and the Prospects for 1982* (St. George's, Grenada: 1982), p. 22.

29. Ibid., p. 23.

30. Maurice Bishop, "Together We Shall Build Our Airport," March 29, 1981, in Bruce Marcus and Michael Taber (eds.), *Maurice Bishop Speaks: The Grenada Revolution 1979–1983* (New York: Pathfinder Press, 1983), p. 143.

31. *Maurice Bishop Speaks to U.S. Workers*, June 5, 1983 (New York: Pathfinder Press, 1983), p. 30.

32. Frank Taylor, *Jamaica — The Welcoming Society, Myths and Reality*, Working Paper No. 8 (Kingston, Jamaica: Institute of Social and Economic Research, 1975), pp. 40–41.

33. V.S. Naipaul, *The Middle Passage, The Caribbean Revisited* (London: Penguin Books, 1969), p. 210.

34. Fitzroy Ambursley, "Grenada: The New Jewel Revolution," in Fitzroy Ambursley and Robin Cohen (eds.), *Crisis in the Caribbean* (New York: Monthly Review Press, 1983), p. 219.

35. Bernard Coard, *Report on the National Economy for 1981 and the Prospects for 1982*, p. 46.

36. United Nations, Economic Commission for Latin America, Office for the Caribbean, *Agricultural Statistics, Vols. IV and V, 1982*, Table 4.8, p. 27.

37. Ibid., Table 6, p. 38.

38. Ibid., Table 6, p. 38.

39. Bernard Coard, *Report on the National Economy*, p. 46.

40. Alister McIntyre, "Adjustments of Caribbean Economies to Changing International Relations," in Lloyd B. Rankine (ed.), *Proceedings of the Sixteenth West Indies Agricultural Economics Conference*, p. 19. For contributions to this debate see, D. Noel and G.I. Marecheau, "A Strategy for Development of Small-Scale Farming in the Commonwealth Caribbean with Special Reference to Grenada," in *Proceedings of the Fifth West Indies Agricultural Economics Conference* (Trinidad: University of the West Indies, 1970).

41. L.G. Campbell, "Strategy for Maximizing Self-Sufficiency in Food in the Region," in S.C. Birla (ed.), *Proceedings of the Tenth West Indies Agricultural Economics Conference*, Vol. I: *Plenary Papers* (Trinidad: University of the West Indies, 1971), p. 59.

42. Bernard Coard, *Report on the National Economy*, pp. 46, 49, 50–51.

43. Bernard Coard, "Extract from Comrade Coard's Speech: Report on the National Economy for 1981 and the Prospects for 1982," in *To Construct from Morning: Making the People's Budget in Grenada* (St. George's, Grenada: Fedon Publishers, 1982), p. 118.

44. "Central Committee Resolution on Agriculture (Confidential)," Control No. 100310, p. 1. This source is part of the papers and documents discovered by U.S. troops in Grenada which were subsequently released by the U.S. Department of State.

45. The World Bank estimated that in 1988 the government controlled 80 percent of the recorded import and export trade and 85 percent of total investment. See The World Bank, *Guyana: From Economic Recovery to Sustained Growth* (Washington, DC: The World Bank, 1993), p. 3.

46. DeLisle Worrell, *Small Island Economies* p. 84.

47. Ibid., pp. 89, 91.

48. Clive Y. Thomas, *The Poor and the Powerless: Economic Policy and Change in the Caribbean* (New York: Monthly Review Press, 1988), pp. 260, 261.

49. DeLisle Worrell, *Small Island Economies*, p. 99.

50. Ibid., p. 100.

51. The World Bank, *Guyana: From Economic Recovery to Sustained Growth*, p. 3.

52. Norman Girvan, "Comment on Thomas' Paper," in George Beckford and Norman Girvan (eds.), *Development in Suspense: Selected Papers and Proceedings of the First Conference of Caribbean Economists* (Kingston, Jamaica: Friedrich Ebert Stiftung, 1989), p. 317.

53. The World Bank, *Caribbean Region: Current Economic Situation, Regional Issues and Capital Flows, 1992* (Washington, DC: The World Bank, 1993), p. 114.

54. For a brief discussion of the relationship between the World Bank, IMF and Jamaica see Dennis Pantin, *Into the Valley of Debt: An Alternative Road to the IMF/World Bank Path* (Trinidad: Dennis Pantin, 1989), pp. 20–22.

55. In Cordella Charlton's study of this period the same conclusion is reached. Charlton writes, "the negative impact of adjustment strategies on both public and private investment was evident throughout the analysis." See Cordella Charlton, "Investment Patterns and Economic Growth in Jamaica: 1981–1988," *Working Paper Series No. 118* (The Hague: Institute of Social Studies, 1992), p. 53.

CHAPTER 7

Natural Endowments and Economic Development

In this chapter we take up a group of countries which upon first examination seem to be very different from each other. Trinidad and Tobago is the second largest of the nations examined in this study and by far possesses the highest per capita income in the region. It long has occupied this pinnacle position because it is the sole nation in the region to export petroleum products. Antigua and Barbuda, Barbados, Dominica, St. Kitts and Nevis, St. Lucia and St. Vincent and the Grenadines in contrast are all much smaller and poorer than Trinidad and Tobago. None of them exports a raw material or a processed natural resource. Either the cultivation of bananas or the providing of tourism constitutes the base of their economies, sectors of the economy which are of little importance in Trinidad and Tobago.

Despite such differences, these countries share two characteristics which make their comparison potentially fruitful. First, each of them employed an economic development strategy which most economists would endorse. On the basis of the natural resources which they possessed, each attempted to identify the industry for which it possessed a comparative advantage. Its approach to development then was to concentrate on these industries, antici- pating that in doing so and importing other goods for consumption, it would be able to maximize its income. In this grouping, in short, the doctrine of comparative advantage was followed. In Trinidad and Tobago, this meant encouraging industries which were linked to its petroleum and natural gas endowments. In the rest of the Eastern Caribbean, tourism suggested itself insofar as the sea and beaches were thought of as natural resources.

Second, these countries did not experiment with socialist forms during the 1970s and 1980s. Though Trinidad and Tobago experienced an attempted black power insurrection in 1970 and a 1992 Muslim fundamentalist uprising and there was political unrest in St. Lucia and Dominica in the 1970s, by and large these nations represent the territories of relative political stability in the region. To be sure, as we shall see, even in these relatively conservative states, the government adopted an activist and growth-promoting role. Nonetheless since independence, none of these nations has articulated an ideological position seeking the kinds of goals which were adopted by the socialists of Jamaica, Guyana, and Grenada.

These countries, then, represent a test of the view that development can best promote prosperity by adhering to the doctrine of comparative advantage in a context of political stability.

TRINIDAD AND TOBAGO 1973–90

The most fortunately placed of these countries was Trinidad and Tobago. As an oil producing country, though not a member of the Organization of Petroleum Exporting Countries (OPEC), it became the beneficiary of the huge increase in petroleum prices which occurred in 1973–74 and then again in 1979–80. The revenue generated from this source eliminated, at least in the short run, financing as a constraint to the country's economic development. In Trinidad and Tobago the question of development centered chiefly on whether the society would deploy its new found wealth in a way to expand its capacity to produce a diversified and increased level of output.

The magnitude and rapidity of Trinidad and Tobago's economic gain as a result of the increase in petroleum prices, borders on the unbelievable. Between 1971 and 1974 petroleum's contribution to the Gross Domestic Product increased more than fivefold, from about $(TT) 350 million to over 1.8 billion. Between 1974 and 1977 this statistic increased again by 72 percent to 3.2 billion. After a one year dip the second price spike was experienced and petroleum's contribution to the economy more than doubled once again to 6.7 billion. Thus overall between the 1971 trough and the 1980 peak, petroleum revenues increased almost twenty-fold.

Thereafter, however, the trend in petroleum export earnings was downward. By 1983 petroleum revenues were only about three-quarters of the level they had reached in the peak year. Furthermore they continued a steady downward movement reaching a low of about 3.6 billion in 1987. While the level reached in that year was far higher than that of the early 1970s it still was the case that petroleum's contribution to Trinidad and Tobago's economy had declined by about 46 percent between 1980 and 1987. These

Table 1

Petroleum Industry Contribution to Gross Domestic Product at Factor Cost, and Gross Domestic Product Per Capita in 1987 prices, 1971–86 (millions of $TT)

Year	Petroleum contribution to GDP	Gross domestic product per capita
1971	347.0	14338
1972	414.4	14880
1973	682.8	15107
1974	1,839.0	15789
1975	2,299.8	15943
1976	2,611.0	17280
1977	3,169.3	18129
1978	3,041.8	19976
1979	4,392.4	20588
1980	6,664.4	21928
1981	6,286.1	22581
1982	5,411.1	20954
1983	4,645.7	19039
1984	4,972.1	16644
1985	4,819.2	15580
1986	3,719.9	15071
1987	3,579.8	14191

Sources: Petroleum Contribution to GDP: Central Bank of Trinidad and Tobago, *Handbook of Key Economic Statistics* (Port of Spain, Trinidad: Central Bank of Trinidad and Tobago, 1989), Table A3, pp. 8–11; Gross Domestic Product Per Capita: Computed from The World Bank, *World Tables, 1993* (Washington, DC: The World Bank, 1993), pp. 604–605.

dramatic decreases in petroleum earnings had their counterpart in the country's real GDP per capita. According to the World Bank, Trinidad and Tobago's GDP per capita, adjusted for inflation, increased from $(TT) 14,338 in 1971 to a peak of 22,581 in 1981. Paralleling the movement in petroleum, however, this statistic steadily declined to 14,191 in 1987 and a low of 12,954 in 1990.[1]

The era of extraordinary growth was short lived. Petroleum had gone through a boom and bust. The problem was that the economy did not become sufficiently diversified to pick up the slack once the petroleum crest had receded. Indeed through the boom years, 1974 to the early 1980's, agricultural production actually declined by 16 percent. Similarly, though the value of manufacturing output tended to increase during the petroleum boom, even at its peak, in 1980, the value of manufacturing had increased by only 15.8 percent compared to the 1973 level. In the latter year manufacturing contributed only about 16 percent of the country's output, a percentage which in subsequent years was to decline markedly.[2]

The Government had wanted the outcome of the petroleum boom to be different. While it shared the views of academic commentators, such as Andrew S. Richter, that the Trinidadian private sector was too weak to be the agent of industrialization, Government officials argued that the government itself would be able to promote industrial development. Richter argued that Trinidadian businessmen had exhibited a very cautious attitude toward investment, never straying very far from their initial mercantile interests. He acknowledged that the huge capital outlays required in the petroleum sector were beyond their capacities. But even in smaller scale manufacturing, Richter wrote, "local business interest goes no further than the same low local value-added import-substituting assembly project." As he put it, "industrialism cannot proceed without industrialists."[3] More recently a prominent Trinidadian economist agreed with this assessment. Frank Rampersad at a recent conference argued that "the indigenous entrepreneurial class is not extensively populated by risk takers in the Schumpeterian sense; by and large, indigenous investors have not demonstrated a willingness to extend the frontiers of production."[4] Under the circumstances, the Trinidad and Tobago Government concluded that if industrialization were to occur it would have to be done under the leadership of the public sector. As Rampersad put it, "In these circumstances State participation in industrial and commercial activity is not only justifiable, it is necessary."[5]

Hope for success in public sector industrialization rested on two grounds. First, petroleum had provided the financial resources to carry out large-scale investment projects. As the Prime Minister of the country, Dr. Eric Williams, is reputed to have remarked, with the petroleum boom "money is no problem" for the public sector.[6] Second, the energy sector could enable the Government to create industries which would be competitive in world markets. While petroleum provided revenue and therefore financing, it was natural gas which, it was hoped, would create the foundation for industries in which Trinidad and Tobago would possess a comparative advantage. In light of the fact that energy was relatively inexpensive and abundant in the country, it was believed that energy intensive industries could prosper. Thus, the anticipation was that government could do what the private sector was not able to do: conceive and finance a strategy of large-scale capital investments which would allow Trinidad and Tobago successfully to industrialize.

Natural gas is often present in the same locations as crude oil. This has long been the case in Trinidad and Tobago, but it was not until 1968 that very large reserves of natural gas were discovered and the government set about the task of determining how best to exploit the potential which these holdings represented. In the mid-1970s it was decided that a pipeline would be constructed to bring the natural gas to a new industrial site at Point Lisas. There, five new factories would be constructed for the production of outputs which either used natural gas as an input or were energy intensive. To be produced at Point Lisas was ammonia, urea, methanol and iron billets and rods. Thus it was that Prime Minister Eric Williams on the day that new construction of the industrial site began declared that at last Trinidad and Tobago had broken with its plantation past and that "here at Point Lisas, sugar cane gives way to iron rods."[7]

Government investment was not confined to Point Lisas and the energy-based industries erected there. Using revenue from petroleum, the Government became the principle investor and owner of a range of industries which, in Trevor Farrell's words, "staggers the unfamiliar." Farrell reported that in the early 1980s the public sector owned, either wholly or as the majority shareholders, 53 enterprises and maintained minority shareholding status in an additional 11 firms. In 1984 state-owned companies employed 23,000 persons and majority-owned companies employed 9,000. These 32,000 employment opportunities, when added to the civil service which employed 50,000, meant that the Government was responsible for about one-fifth of all jobs present in the country.[8]

It was, however, the Point Lisas facility which was the key to the industrialization effort. Thus it was that its failure to be profitable was a decisive setback in the country's attempt to achieve modern economic growth. Dennis A. Pantin has studied the Point Lisas experience, and though he cautions repeatedly that what he provides are only estimates, his nonetheless represents the best analysis so far available.

Table 2

Cumulative Profitability of Natural Gas Based Industries at Point Lisas, 1982–86 ($TT 000)

Company	Product	% gov't equity	Profit (loss) per year
Tringen II	Ammonia	51	35.3
ISCOTT	Iron and steel	100	(1132.7)
Fertrin	Ammonia	51	(227.0)
T&T Urea Co.	Urea	100	(106.7)
T&T Methanol Co.	Methanol	100	(125.7)
Total			(1556.8)

Source: Denis A. Pantin, "Whither Pt. Lisas?: Lessons for the Future," Table 2, p. 31, and Table 4, p. 33.

As can be seen in Table 2, four of the five firms involved experienced substantial losses in their first five years in production. In the aggregate their combined losses over this period came to more than $(TT) 1.5 billion. In incurring these losses, Pantin differentiates between the experiences of the ammonia, urea and methanol producers and that of the iron and steel company. The former, Pantin believes, were relatively efficient in production, but suffered because of adverse movements in world market prices. Iron and steel too suffered from declining prices, but this company (ISCOTT) experienced major production problems as well. As Pantin writes, "ISCOTT has not been able to get its production act together" and as a result production costs were higher than they should have been to effectively compete in world markets. The disappointment associated with this entire project is revealed in Pantin's remark that "the real issue is whether the sector which was supposed to carry the rest of the economy can now be carried by the latter."[9]

Because of the debacle at Point Lisas the Government was not successful in stimulating a structural transformation of the country's economy. It actively was investing in businesses hoping that by using the country's abundant energy sources and by producing petroleum and natural gas based products it could find a viable path to industrialization. But the commercial

Table 3

Sectoral Contribution to Gross Domestic Product at Factor Cost, 1970–86 (Percent)

Year	Petroleum	Agriculture	Manufacturing	Other
1970	23.0	6.4	9.9	60.7
1975	44.1	4.9	6.2	44.8
1980	42.8	3.2	5.9	48.1
1986	21.8	5.7	8.2	64.3
1990	24.1	2.7	8.7	64.5

Sources: 1970–86: Calculated from Central Bank of Trinidad and Tobago, *Handbook of Key Economic Statistics* (Trinidad and Tobago: Central Bank of Trinidad and Tobago, 1989), Table A3, pp. 10–11; 1990: Calculated from Central Bank of Trinidad and Tobago, *Annual Economic Survey 1992* (Trinidad and Tobago: Central Bank of Trinidad and Tobago, 1992), Table A.2 (no page).

weaknesses of the Point Lisas firms limited the extent to which they became the foundation for an expansion of the country's manufacturing sector.

The result was that when petroleum revenue fell in the 1980s, the manufacturing sector was not able to offset the impact of that decline. This is revealed in Table 3 which provides information on the relative importance of the principle sectors of Trinidad and Tobago's economy. The petroleum boom is revealed in the doubling of the relative importance of that sector which occurred in 1975 and 1980. But by 1986 and 1990 it had returned to a contribution comparable to that of 1970. The big disappointment was the fact that manufacturing's contribution had not increased at all, still remaining at a level of less than 10 percent of the country's gross domestic product. Obviously the government had not done well in its role as principle industrial entrepreneur.

Farrell, in reviewing the experience in the Caribbean generally, identifies bureaucratic red tape, featherbedding and the availability of subsidies from the national treasury as the reasons for the government's weaknesses in business and commercial activities. With regard to the first, "the speed and decisions often required for successful commercial operations" were frequently absent. To that inefficiency was added overstaffing, the result of pressures to provide jobs for politically loyal constituents. Finally, the penalty for the resulting inefficiencies was limited by what in the circumstances of the former Soviet Union was described as a "soft budget constraint." The ready availability of subsidies from the national treasury meant that failures in the market place did not "bring the swift retribution of bankruptcy or shareholder revolt which the ordinary commercial enterprise has to face."[10] Under the circumstances loss-earning public enterprises became the rule, with the upshot being that little sustained industrial development was generated.

The lost income associated with the end of the petroleum boom required a decline in imports if Trinidad and Tobago were to avoid mounting indebtedness. This adjustment, however, was slow in coming. As indicated in Table 4, the country's positive current account, its excess of exports over imports allowed it to enjoy an overall surplus in its balance of payments throughout the period from 1974 to 1981. The decline in the value of petroleum exports in the early 1980s, however, was not matched either by a fall in imports or an acceleration in the flow of capital to the country. As a result its balance of payments fell seriously negative in 1983 and continued so through 1987.

The fact that in 1988 the country entered into agreements with the International Monetary Fund to restructure its debt signalled the failure of its state-dependent industrialization strategy. A major element in all agreements entered into by the IMF to assist an indebted country is that it liberalize its economy and reduce the role of the government in it. Thus when Trinidad and Tobago turned to the IMF, a major chapter in its economic history had come to an end. The government no longer was to be looked to as the agent of modern economic development.

TOURIST DEVELOPMENT

What Antigua and Barbuda, Barbados, Dominica, St. Kitts and Nevis, St. Lucia, and St. Vincent and the Grenadines most profoundly share with each other and what most decisively influences their potential for economic development is smallness of size. The largest of them, Barbados, in 1970 possessed a population of less than 250,000; none of the others contained as many as 200,000. Combined, Antigua, Dominica, St. Kitts, St. Lucia and St. Vincent and the Grenadines possessed a population of only about 365,000.[11]

Even more than is the case for Jamaica, Guyana, and Trinidad and Tobago, this shared smallness of size necessitates that these economies be extensive participants in international trade. Limited resources, including labor, preclude any one of the islands from producing a wide array of goods and services. There simply are not enough workers or other inputs on any one

Table 4

Balance of Payments, Trinidad and Tobago, 1974–87 ($TT 000)

Year	Current account	Capital account	Errors and omissions	Overall surplus/ deficit
1974	576.0	67.9	–41.3	602.6
1975	715.9	334.7	–94.3	956.3
1976	618.5	–25.9	–107.1	485.5
1977	414.5	685.1	–39.9	1059.7
1978	97.1	699.7	–38.8	758.0
1979	–87.0	1021.1	–55.0	879.1
1980	1132.3	394.1	–53.9	1472.5
1981	956.4	526.7	–117.5	1365.6
1982	–1615.7	975.1	115.9	–524.7
1983	–2464.0	248.0	53.5	–2162.5
1984	–1336.4	–60.6	–351.5	–1749.0
1985	–263.4	327.7	–325.9	–261.6
1986	–2275.0	67.6	–180.1	–2387.5
1986	–974.7	–115.5	174.3	–915.9

Source: Central Bank of Trinidad and Tobago, *Handbook of Key Economic Statistics* (Trinidad and Tobago: Central Bank of Trinidad and Tobago, 1989), Table B.1, p. 131.

island to permit a diverse pattern of production. The small size of the population also means that the domestic market of any of these countries is very limited. Virtually any industry will require a greater level of demand than is domestically present to achieve productive efficiencies. In the absence of some form of economic integration, these supply and demand constraints imposed by smallness of size, require that nearly all consumer needs be imported. That, in turn, means that for consumer desires to be satisfied, these islands must earn foreign exchange. Thus in seeking economic advance these Eastern Caribbean nations have no choice but to seek out an industry which can service the markets of large, already developed countries.

In the Eastern Caribbean, conventional industrial raw materials are all but unavailable. Only Barbados possesses a limited amount of petroleum but even in this case it is not available in large enough quantities to export. In short, none of these countries is able to earn foreign exchange as Jamaica and Guyana do by exporting bauxite or Trinidad and Tobago does by exporting petroleum and petroleum products. Only Antigua and Barbuda for a period of time possessed a petroleum refinery, but that facility processed crude which was imported.

But though conventionally defined natural resources are not present in the region, all but Dominica and perhaps St. Vincent and the Grenadines do possess the natural endowments associated with international tourism. In much of the Eastern Caribbean, the region's tropical climate is joined with sandy beaches and moderate surf to provide the basis upon it could claim a comparative advantage for a foreign exchange earning tourist industry. Until rapid and relatively inexpensive travel became available, the potential which climate and sea represented was largely untapped. But once jet planes came to be employed extensively by commercial airlines in the 1950s and 1960s, the development of a tourist industry became commercially feasible. With incomes rising in the countries in which the region's tourism would be marketed — mainly the United States, Canada and Great Britain — the demand side of the market experienced a long-term upward trend. Furthermore tourism marketed in this way could become a foreign exchange-earning industry. Tourism, in short, suggested itself as a sector in which the region should specialize.

As indicated in Table 5, Antigua, followed by Barbados, was the pioneer of tourism in the region. Paget Henry writes that when members of Antigua's Industrial Development Board passed a Hotel Aid Ordinance in 1952, "never in their wildest imaginings did the members ... ever seriously anticipate the possibility that the growth in international travel and the 1959 Revolution in Cuba would conspire to make tourism the major industry of the island."[12] However, annual tourist arrivals as early as 1958 came to about one-fourth the population size of the island and five years later were almost 80 percent of Antigua's population. Such relative levels were not experienced in the neighboring islands until the mid-1970s. Even Barbados did not approximate Antigua's 1963 relative tourist industry size until 1972.

Edsil Phillips reports that well into the 1960s the Barbados tourist industry catered to "a small group of wealthy North Americans who had become accustomed to spending winter in a warm climate."[13] Its small scale was

Table 5

Tourist Arrivals Per Capita, Selected West Indian Nations, 1958–87

	1958	1963	1968	1972	1978	1982	1987
Antigua	0.24	0.79	0.85	1.10	1.71	2.31	4.49
Barbados	0.11	0.22	0.49	0.88	1.52	1.70	2.41
Dominica	NA	NA	0.14	0.22	NA	0.30	0.49
St. Kitts	NA	NA	0.22	0.36	0.52	1.06	2.26
St. Lucia	NA	NA	0.22	0.42	1.24	0.92	1.51
St. Vincent	NA	NA	0.14	0.19	0.57	0.70	0.85

Sources: Tourist Arrivals: Antigua, 1958, 1968, Paget Henry, *Peripheral Capitalism and Underdevelopment in Antigua* (New Brunswick: Transaction Books, 1958), Table 4.3, p. 123; Barbados, 1958, 1963, Edsil Phillips, "The Development of the Tourist Industry in Barbados, 1956–1980," in DeLisle Worrell, ed., *The Economy of Barbados, 1946–1980* (Bridgetown, Barbados: Central Bank of Barbados, 1982), Table 1, p. 109. All others except 1968 Antigua: Sidney E. Chernick, *The Commonwealth Caribbean: The Integration Experience* (Baltimore: The Johns Hopkins University Press, 1978), Table SA9.1, p. 464. All countries, 1978, 1982 and 1987: The World Bank, *Caribbean Countries: Economic Situation, Regional Issues and Capital Flows* (Washington, DC: The World Bank, 1988), Table 1.5, p. 69. Population: Caribbean Community Secretariat, *Caribbean Development to the Year 2000: Challenges, Prospects and Policies* (Georgetown, Guyana: Caribbean Community Secretariat, 1988), Table II.2, p. 130.

reflected in its per capita tourist arrival rate of less than one-half that experienced in Antigua in 1953. As in the latter country, Barbados' industry started to grow when tax and other concessions were offered to it in a Hotel Aids Act of 1956 and the Government established a Barbados Tourist Board in 1958. That agency, in turn, was important in shifting the industry to a more mass consumer base especially through its promotional campaigns.[14] The tourist arrival rate thereafter approximately doubled every five years until finally the industry growth rate slowed in the 1980s.

In the 1970s and 1980s, St. Kitts and Nevis and St. Lucia joined Antigua and Barbuda, and Barbados as countries with rapidly growing tourist indus-

Table 6

**Gross Domestic Product Per Capita (EC$) and Percent
Sectoral Contributions to Output, 1970**

Country	GDP per capita	Export agricul- ture (%)	Manu- fac- turing (%)	Export tourism (%)
Barbados	1232	9.3	10.8	15.5[1]
Antigua	773	3.0	10.2	16.2[2]
St. Kitts	679	15.0	2.7	3.0[2]
St. Lucia	669	16.0	3.6	3.3[2]
Dominica	545	15.4	8.1	6.3[3]
St. Vincent	429	12.9	3.8	3.5[2]

[1]Services. [2]Hotels. [3]Services and professions.

Source: Sidney E. Chernick, *The Commonwealth Caribbean* (Baltimore: The Johns Hopkins University Press, 1978), Tables SA2.2, SA2.6, SA2.7, SA2.10, SA2.11, SA2.12.

tries. Even St. Vincent and the Grenadines and Dominica, countries which are much less favorably endowed with the natural endowments associated with tropical vacations, experienced tourist arrival rates equal to or in excess of one half of their population size. Thus by the 1980s these countries all had become locations where tourism was thriving.

Table 6 ranks these countries by their Gross Domestic Product per capita in 1970. Barbados clearly was the most economically advanced. Its per capita product was 60 percent higher than that of Antigua, the second ranking country. Further, its economy had become much more diversified than the others. Tourism already contributed more to output than the traditional export crop, sugar, and manufacturing too made a 10 percent contribution to production. Among the others, Antigua had moved the furthest from the region's historic dependence on export agriculture. There too tourism was the single largest productive sector. The presence of an oil refinery was responsible for manufacturing's relatively strong role in the economy. Elsewhere, however, little structural change had been experienced. Export agriculture, sugar in the case of St. Kitts and bananas elsewhere continued to

Table 7

Percentage Change in Real Gross Domestic Product, 1971–80 and 1981–90

	1971–80	1981–90
Barbados	28.4	11.7
Antigua	6.2	80.9
St. Kitts	20.0	66.3
St. Lucia	26.2	50.6
Dominica	–24.5	45.7
St. Vincent	10.8	80.2

Sources: 1971–80: Antigua, Dominica, St. Kitts, St. Lucia, St. Vincent, Arnold M. McIntyre, *The Economies of the Organisation of Eastern Caribbean States in the 1970s*, Occasional Paper No. 18 (Cave Hill, Barbados: Institute of Social and Economic Research (Eastern Caribbean), 1986), Table 2, p. 46; Barbados, The World Bank, *World Tables 1993* (Washington, DC: The World Bank, 1993), 1981–90: Central Bank of Barbados, *Annual Statistical Digest 1991* (Barbados: The Central Bank of Barbados, 1991), Table J11, p. 208, and Table I1, p. 170.

dominate production. Neither tourism nor manufacturing had as yet emerged as substantial sources of production.

As indicated in Table 7, each of these countries, excepting Barbados, experienced more rapid economic growth during the 1980s than the 1970s. The three most dramatic changes in fortune occurred in Antigua and Barbuda, Dominica, and St. Vincent and the Grenadines. But even in St. Kitts and Nevis and in St. Lucia, where the change in trend was less dramatic, growth during the 1980s was just about twice the level reached in the 1970s. In Barbados, however, the reverse was experienced. Economic growth during the later decade was less than half the rate experienced in the earlier one.

Despite the oil shocks and the severe recession experienced in the United States in the mid-1970s, Barbados experienced a growth in its economy of more than 2.5% per year during that decade. Tourist arrivals in the country more than doubled between 1970 and 1979, increasing from 156,000 to 371,000. This increase was far greater than the growth in the tourist industry which occurred in other vacation destinations such as the Bahamas, Bermuda, Jamaica or the countries of the Eastern Caribbean. Tourist expenditures in Barbados grew even more rapidly than did arrivals. In current prices, outlays by vacationing visitors almost doubled in the years 1970–74 alone and increased by fivefold during the decade.[15] Tourism, in short, boomed in Barbados in the 1970s.

Manufacturing too grew substantially in these years, though not as rapidly as tourism. Manufacturing's contribution to gross domestic product, in real terms, increased from $(B) 191 million in 1971 to almost $(B) 320 million in 1979, increasing from 10.3 percent of the country's output to 14.1 percent. Only agriculture failed to grow during these years. Agriculture's contribution to GDP was $(B) 243.0 million in 1971, a level which exceeded the annual average attained throughout the decade by about 15 percent. This stagnation in agriculture, however, was barely noticed since the growth in tourism and manufacturing resulted in a dramatic increase in the country's output. According to the World Bank, Barbados' gross national income in real terms grew at a very healthy rate of almost 3 percent per year during the decade of the 1970s.[16]

In contrast, the growth rate of the Barbados economy declined to only about 1 percent per year between 1980 and 1990. Table 8 reveals what happened. Sugar production experienced a catastrophic decline in production of 42 percent, a fall which the rest of the agricultural sector failed to offset. Manufacturing too declined in these years, so that the 1990–91 level of output was 8 percent lower than it had been ten years earlier. The single biggest source of this fall occurred in the production of electronic components. Following the shutting down of a United States based firm, production in this sector all but ground to a halt.[17] Finally, the tourist industry was hurt by a substantial decrease in the number of days visitors stayed in the country. Between 1974 and 1981 the average length of stay of tourists to Barbados stood at a peak level of 9.1 days. But in the ten years thereafter the average length of stay fell by 23.1 percent to 7.0 days. As a result, even though tourist arrivals continued to rise, earnings in the tourist industry were only 1.6 percent higher in the second period than in the first.[18]

The decline in manufacturing and export agriculture and the very slow growth experienced in tourism during the late 1980s and early 1990s resulted in a deterioration in the country's international current account. Its excess of imports compared to exports resulted in a rapid decline in its holdings of foreign exchange, so that by September 1991 these holdings were all but depleted. As a result Barbados entered into an eighteen-month stabilization program with the International Monetary Fund, whose purpose was to restore equilibrium in its international trade by cutting back on imports and

Table 8

Barbados Economy: Output by Sector, 1980/81–1990/91 ($B million in 1974 prices)

Sector	1980–81	1982–83	1984–85	1986–87	1988–89	1990–91
Sugar	49.6	37.2	42.5	41.2	31.2	28.8
Other agriculture	25.9	30.9	33.2	33.2	31.8	34.5
Manufacturing	93.1	87.6	86.1	83.2	88.0	85.5
Construction	57.6	51.5	50.3	55.2	64.4	57.9
Tourism	107.3	88.2	92.0	104.1	129.3	118.7
Government	103.0	101.1	104.4	114.0	118.0	119.1
Other	358.1	353.4	374.3	406.7	430.6	417.0
Total	794.6	749.9	782.8	837.6	893.3	861.5

Source: Calculated from Central Bank of Barbados, *Annual Statistical Digest, 1992* (Barbados: The Central Bank of Barbados, 1992), Table I1, p. 170.

stimulating exports. This was to be accomplished through an austerity program which involved among other items a decrease in the wage bill for public sector employees, a reduction in spending on capital projects, increased taxation and a reduction in private sector credit.[19]

In contrast to the experience in Barbados, the 1980s was a decade of economic growth for Antigua and Barbuda, Dominica, St. Kitts and Nevis, St. Lucia, and St. Vincent and the Grenadines. Given the narrow structure of production in these countries, this economic advance is easily identifiable. What happened in the tourist industry and in export agriculture was decisive in determining the pattern of change in these countries. In both, the trend was favorable.

Each of the five countries experienced a dramatic increase in gross revenues generated by the tourist industry. By far the most successful, Antigua and Barbuda, experienced an increase in its annual revenue of almost $(US) 100 million between 1977/81 and 1982/87. The second largest increase occurred in St. Lucia, though proportionately Dominica's growth was even more dramatic. In the latter country, however, the lack of the natural

Table 9

Tourist Arrivals and Expenditures, 1977/81–1982/87

	1977/81			1982/87		
	(1)	(2)	(3)	(1)	(2)	(3)
	Arrivals 1000s	Expenditures mill. $US	Expenditures per arrival	Arrivals 1000s	Expenditures mill. $US	Expenditures per arrival
Antigua	163.4	35.3	216	242.0	133.5	551
St. Kitts	40.6[1]	7.4[1]	182[1]	72.9	18.7	256
Dominica	28.4	3.1	109	28.5	9.1	319
St. Lucia	133.0	27.5	206	134.1[2]	40.5[2]	302[2]
St. Vincent	57.4	12.1	210	79.5[2]	16.6[2]	208[2]

[1]1978–81. [2]1982–86.

Source: Calculated from The World Bank, *Caribbean Countries: Economic Situation, Regional Issues and Capital Flows* (Washington, DC: The World Bank, 1988), Tables 1.4 and 1.5, pp. 68, 69.

endowments associated with tourism limited its relative contribution to the economy (see Table 9).

Table 9 indicates that Antigua and Barbuda benefitted from the fact that while tourist arrivals to the country increased by 48 percent, expenditures per arrival were two and a half time greater in 1982/87 than in 1977/81. A similar, but less dramatic trend occurred in St. Kitts and Nevis. Elsewhere however, one or the other, but not both, increased. Dominica and St. Lucia saw per tourist expenditures rise dramatically, tripling in the first country and increasing by nearly 50 percent in the second. But in both, the mean arrival rate remained flat. In contrast arrivals in St. Vincent increased by almost 40 percent but expenditures per tourist remained stable.

Aside from Antigua and Barbuda, each of these countries possessed an important agricultural staple industry as well as tourism. St. Kitts and Nevis continued to produce sugar but that industry's deteriorating performance acted as a brake on the advance stimulated by tourism. The fall in production and earnings which are reported in Table 10 occurred in the context of what a visiting delegation from the World Bank described as "a variety of different crises."[20] The guaranteed market which St. Kitts enjoyed for its sugar under

Table 10

Banana and Sugar Exports and Revenues, 1977/81–1982/87

	1977/81			1982/87		
	(1)	(2)	(3)	(1)	(2)	(3)
	Tons (1000s)	Revenue mill. US$	Revenue per ton	Tons (1000s)	Revenue mill. US$	Revenue per ton
Bananas						
Dominica	23.7	6.5	274	39.5	17.1	433
St. Lucia	42.6	12.1	284	73.5	31.2	424
St. Vincent	25.6	7.0	273	33.1[2]	13.7[2]	413[2]
Sugar						
St. Kitts	33.4[1]	13.1[1]	392[1]	26.0	10.4	400

[1]1978/81. [2]1982/86.

Source: Calculated from The World Bank, *Caribbean Countries: Economic Situation, Regional Issues and Capital Flows* (Washington, DC: The World Bank, 1988), Tables 1.8, 1.9, 1.6, 1.7, pp. 70–73.

the Lome Convention did not offer prices high enough to cover its rising production costs. Field and factory operations were described in favorable terms by the World Bank. However, the Bank's representatives complained about the industry's poor managerial performance, especially as it dealt with labor relations and the supervision of field operations. Writing in 1984 the Bank declared that the loss which the industry was incurring "casts doubts upon the long-run viability of the sector."[21]

In the Windward Islands of Dominica, St. Lucia and St. Vincent and the Grenadines, by the mid-1960s bananas had become the agricultural staple. Sugar had never been of overwhelming importance in Dominica and had been abandoned in St. Vincent and the Grenadines in 1962 and in St. Lucia in 1964.[22] In St. Vincent and the Grenadines however, much of the land formerly used in cane was unsuited for banana cultivation. In contrast, virtually all of the former sugar land in St. Lucia, though not ideal for the crop, could be used in bananas. For that reason this peasant-grown crop came to dominate agriculture in that country in much the same way that sugar had done so in an earlier era.

All Windward Island bananas are marketed by a single firm — Geest Industries — based in Great Britain. Most of the bananas are cultivated by small farmers. These individual cultivators sell their output to the local producers' association which, in turn, sells the bananas to Geest. Geest literally fills a monopsonist role as the single buyer of the staple, a position which has caused much unfavorable comment. Thus Troillot, for example, writes that "neither the association nor the peasants has any bargaining power in determining the conditions of each transaction, the volume involved, the quantity or quality of the accepted fruits." What exists is only "the illusion of a price." In fact, according to Trouillot, banana producers are completely dominated by Geest and receive only payment for their labor. In his words, "Dominican yeomen and tenants are in fact working in their own gardens for a British-based transnational corporation."[23]

But while this may be true, the fact is that the banana industry in the Windwards has flourished. With Geest's shipping, ripening and marketing competence, and a market in which the region's bananas are provided with preferential access, the banana industry has grown dramatically. Even the Latin American Bureau, a severe critic of multinational corporations, acknowledges that during the 1980s a "boom in banana production has created a substantial influx of export earnings into the Windward Islands, most notably in St. Lucia, and has resulted in large increases in income for farmers." The result has been "a rapid expansion in private consumption, as farmers have more cash to spend on goods, most of which are imported. Cars, televisions and other consumer durables have poured into the islands."[24]

The banana industry is a small farm industry. In St. Lucia, for example, average farm size is estimated to be only five to ten acres with over 75 percent of the plots of 10 acres or less. Expanding the acreage under bananas is all but impossible since already by the mid-1980s 71 percent of St. Lucia's arable land was under banana.[25] Furthermore, the industry is not really competitive by world standards. Farmers cultivate bananas profitably only because their output is sold in a guaranteed market in the United Kingdom.

One problem in this regard is that yields are low. In part this is so because the land is not ideal for banana cultivation. To make things worse, it is unlikely that yields will increase significantly even with increased use of fertilizers. The World Bank estimates that the average yield per acre in St. Lucia is 5–6 tons compared to 10–15 tons in neighboring Martinique and Guadeloupe.[26] Together all of this means that if the protection the industry receives in the United Kingdom were to be reduced or eliminated, banana cultivation would experience a dramatic contraction. As presently structured, the banana industry clearly is not the kind of industry which can lead the Windwards to modern economic growth.

The question then which remains is the extent to which tourism can be expected to propel the Eastern Caribbean towards economic modernization. As we saw in Chapter 6, this industry has been the object of much local criticism, though some of these comments have been more polemical than analytic. But even Sidney E. Chernick, writing on behalf of the World Bank, agrees that, at least in part, a negative assessment of the industry has "some historical justification."[27] He acknowledges the "social costs which accompany the expansion of tourism — social tension, the alienation of land caused by the movement of small farmers into the tourist labor force, the frustration engendered in the local populace by the lifestyles of affluent visitors and the erosion of dignity and perpetuation of servitude involved in employment in the tourist sector." With regard to strictly economic issues he also concedes that "the income benefits arising from the industry are ... much smaller than they seem. This is the result of very high leakages of earnings from tourist dollars, as expressed in terms of the import costs of inputs ... repatriation of profits on foreign capital, interest payments on foreign loans, and the cost of wages paid to expatriate management personnel."[28] Though the industry, in short, does represent one in which the region has important competitive advantages, it is a sector which has more than its share of disadvantages.

Perhaps even more important than these difficulties, are those concerning the quality of employment opportunities in tourism. For an industry to play a positive role in the economic development experience, it must not only be a source of income and employment. To contribute positively to the development process, it must also create pressure to augment the quality of the labor force. Modern economic development centers on productivity advance, and that in turn, requires skilled and educated workers. Thus if an industry is established which requires well-trained or educated individuals, that demand tends to increase the likelihood that the appropriate level of schooling will be provided. Creating the demand for well-educated workers tends to augment the supply. With that done, the potential for economic growth is increased. But the opposite is the case also. New sectors of economic activity which do not require high quality labor and do not represent the creation of a new pattern of labor demand, do not increase the incentive for such individuals to be trained and become available.

The problem with tourism is that a positive mechanism promoting the increased availability of skilled labor is largely absent. Jost Krippendorf, a leading theorist of tourism, acknowledges that "jobs in tourism are mostly unattractive." Aside from the fact that wages tend to be low and hours irregular, "the range of professional and training possibilities is limited."

Krippendorf goes on, "many jobs are unskilled and considered as socially inferior, for example the work behind the scenes such as in the kitchen or cleaning." Furthermore, as Krippendorf writes, "tourist development projects are hardly ever run by local people. It seems that the natural choice for the good jobs and the demanding managerial posts lies with foreigners and people from the city. The locals are left with the menial jobs and services."[29] Thus far from tourism's exerting a positive pressure to increase the technical competence of the labor force, it, at best, creates jobs for people who remain at skill levels which poorly equip them to participate in the world of modern technology.

Despite the prevailing pessimistic consensus among academic commentators concerning tourism, the industry does have its defenders. Foremost among these is Auliana Poon who argues that "tourism offers the unique opportunity to lead Caribbean economies into a viable, competitive and profitable future." In part Poon argues this is the case because of the strong demand for tourism which can be anticipated in the future. She writes that "unlike many commodities, durable goods and even services, there are not substitutes for the tourism experience." Poon notes that "within the last 25 years tourism has become as much a feature of the 'good' life as a dish washer or a microwave oven" and will continue to do so in the future.[30]

Even so, however, Poon maintains that without major adjustments the region's tourist industry will fail to maximize its contribution to regional development. The current industry Poon describes as the "old tourism," a post–World War II phenomenon which was "standardized and rigidly packaged" and which catered to "sun-lust tourists." She writes, however, that "there are already signs that the tourist industry is beginning to take on a different shape" and that tourists "are moving away from 'tinsel and junk' to more real, natural and authentic experiences."[31]

Poon believes that such a structural change in tourism increases the competitiveness of the Caribbean's industry because it represents a move towards "the real, natural and authentic realms of civilization — the attributes that Caribbean islands can both boast of and offer." Since there is a growing demand "for what the Caribbean has naturally — diversity, authenticity, multicultural forms, etc.," new tourism "provides the opportunities for the Caribbean to complement its product with dignity, environmental quality and conservation." Rather than being passively dependent upon demand patterns in the metropolitan countries, Poon believes that these new developments will mean that "the future of Caribbean tourism will increasingly depend upon its innovativeness — its indigenous capacity to bring new goods, new services and new techniques to the marketplace."[32]

All of this represents a great potential for the region, according to Poon, provided that the isolation of the region's tourist industry from other segments of the service sector is broken down. Her position is that "the future of the Caribbean does not lie in tourism, but in the development of the entire services sector." In this view linkages between tourism and legal and medical services, artists and entertainers, conferences and education and training must be constructed. Caribbean tourists thus could provide a market for an entire array of locally produced services. Her vision is contained in her comments that "there is no reason why the duty-free shopping complexes that have sprung up throughout the Caribbean cannot produce and market dental, health and other services." Acknowledging that "it is difficult for tourism, narrowly defined, to sustain the economic social systems of the Caribbean islands," Poon nevertheless believes that "once tourism is developed in the total services sense, there are a great deal more developmental opportunities to be derived."[33]

There is something to be said about Poon's vision of a future tourism. It makes sense for the region to encourage the industry since it possesses competitive advantages. Poon is right that emphasizing services as contrasted, for example to manufacturing, does not preclude modern economic growth. The service economy can usefully be understood as a "second industrial revolution" and its emergence is, as Poon puts it, "one of the profound developments of the century."[34] And it certainly is true that the demand for tourism will continue to expand in the future and that the region should position itself to take advantage of this growth.

With all of that acknowledged however, there remains grave cause for doubt that Caribbean tourism can become the center of a service sector which caters to the professional needs of visitors. Problems exist on both the demand and the supply side. With regard to the latter the first and most important problem concerns the availability of the trained professionals necessary to supply such services. The number of medical practitioners in the Caribbean is far from the level which would be required for such a scheme to be a success and so is the availability of suitable facilities. At the moment, therefore, the thought that people would come to the Caribbean for medical treatment is laughable. For this strategy to work, the number of physicians and health practitioners would have to be vastly increased as would the stock of capital in the medical care industry. The same would be true for lawyers and other legal practitioners if the law were to be identified as a professional service to be marketed to tourists in the region.

But a bigger problem than the availability of trained professionals concerns demand. Specifically the issue is whether enough visitors to the Caribbean would make the shift from surf and sea to alternative vacations to justify a wholesale reorganization of the industry. It is striking in this regard that Poon, a student of Caribbean tourism, provides no data on this question. Indeed the only justification that she does offer for her projection of growing demand for new tourism is what she says is an estimate by Krippendorf that, by the year 2000, 30–45 percent of the worldwide market will be for the new tourist product. The problem is that Krippendorf does not make such a projection. Rather, he offers the hope that tourism might change in the direction of "a new travel culture." But Krippendorf knows that such a development "is still far from reality. Passive and uncritical tourists still far outnumber active and enlightened ones."[35]

Even if Krippendorf had made such an estimate of worldwide tourist demand, it would have been of little relevance for the Caribbean. The simple fact of the matter is that there is not much evidence that the people who consider coming to the region would make such a shift. The eco-tourism that is currently encouraged in Dominica is minuscule compared to the size of the region's industry. Even more is it difficult to anticipate that on a large scale people in need of health care or legal representation would incur the costs of travelling to the region to secure such professional services.

If there are grounds for skepticism concerning tourism's transforming itself, it nevertheless is the case that much of what Poon advocates is desirable. If Caribbean tourism established stronger links with other sectors of the economy the region would benefit. Imports would be reduced, and domestic production would increase. In the process, employment opportunities would be enhanced. Thus what she says is not so much wrong as excessively optimistic. Shifts in the direction she advocates are desirable. But nothing close to the total transformation she envisions is likely.

In sum, this group of countries — Antigua and Barbuda, Barbados, Dominica, St. Kitts and Nevis, St. Lucia, and St. Vincent and the Grenadines — has not yet embarked on a course leading to their economic modernization. Sugar and bananas are substantial income earners and have proved themselves to be important employment creators. But neither can be expected to be a source of economic modernization. Unfortunately, the same is true of tourism. The region's natural endowments make tourism a logical industry to encourage. Indeed, in the context of an otherwise developed economy, such an industry can serve as a valuable income and employment supplement. But because it employs relatively few skilled and comparatively many unskilled workers, it is not the kind of industry which either characterizes a technologically progressive society or contributes to its construction.

It is true that smallness of size limits the degree to which Caribbean economies can hope to become diversified. Structural change is necessarily minimized. But smallness of size does not imply a limit with regard to the application of modern technology to production. If that is the appropriate criterion to apply in assessing the onset of economic development even in small countries, then what has occurred in the Eastern Caribbean is growth but not development. Incomes have increased because of the expansion of tourism and bananas, but these industries do not possess the characteristics which place a nation on the path of modern economic growth.

CONCLUSION

It is not that Trinidad and the countries of the Eastern Caribbean chose the wrong industries. The natural resources which were available to them suggest that in the context of the doctrine of comparative advantage their choices were sound. Natural gas made energy-based industries attractive in Trinidad and Tobago. The Caribbean's climate endowed it well to provide tourist services.

But the process of economic development does not centrally rest on solving the problem of comparative advantage and selecting the appropriate industrial mix by that standard. Indeed to the extent that the process of modern growth is concerned with comparative advantage at all, it deals with the dynamism of such market positioning. Specifically, advancing technology is what allows countries successfully to compete in markets even when initial factor endowments may make it appear that a particular industry is inappropriate. The right industry, unable to advance technologically, will soon become uncompetitive. The wrong industry, though commercially successful, may not contribute much to the development process.

That is what has happened to the countries which concern us in this chapter. Trinidad may have chosen well, but having done so did not ensure commercial success. Tourism may have been successful in the market, but made little contribution to advancing the people of the region in the direction required by modern economic development.

NOTES

1. Computed from The World Bank, *World Tables 1993*, pp. 604–605.
2. Computed from ibid., pp. 604–605.
3. Andrew S. Richter, "Multinational Corporations, Local Businessmen and the State in a Small Developing Country: A Case Study of Trinidad and Tobago" (unpublished Ph.D. Dissertation, Yale University, 1979), pp. 233, 235.

4. Frank Rampersad, "The Development Experience — Reflections," in Selwyn Ryan (ed.), *Trinidad and Tobago: The Independence Experience, 1962–1987* (St. Augustine, Trinidad and Tobago: The Institute of Social and Economic Research, 1988), p. 15.

5. Ibid., p. 15.

6. As quoted in Scott B. MacDonald, *Trinidad and Tobago: Democracy and Development in the Caribbean* (New York: Praeger Publishers, 1986), p. 191.

7. Selwyn Ryan, "Dr. Eric Williams, the People's National Movement and the Independence Experience: A Retrospective," in Selwyn Ryan (ed.), *Trinidad and Tobago: The Independence Experience*, p. 154.

8. Trevor M.A. Farrell, "The Caribbean State and its Role in Economic Management," in Stanley Lalta and Marie Freckleton (eds.), *Caribbean Economic Development: The First Generation*, pp. 202–203.

9. Dennis A. Pantin, "Whither Pt. Lisas? Lessons for the Future," in Selwyn Ryan (ed.), *Trinidad and Tobago: The Independence Experience*, pp. 35–37, 38.

10. Trevor M.A. Farrell, "The Caribbean State and Its Role in Economic Management," in Stanley Lalta and Marie Freckleton (eds.), *Caribbean Economic Development: The First Generation*, p. 204.

11. Grenada is omitted from consideration here because its development was influenced by its experience with the People's Revolutionary Government. Since the fall of the Maurice Bishop government, its efforts at development have been similar to those discussed in this section.

12. Paget Henry, *Peripheral Capitalism and Underdevelopment in Antigua* (New Brunswick: Transaction Books, 1985), p. 122.

13. Edsil Phillips, "The Development of the Tourist Industry in Barbados, 1956–1980," in DeLisle Worrell (ed.), *The Economy of Barbados, 1946–1980* (Bridgetown: Central Bank of Barbados, 1982), p. 107.

14. Edsil Phillips, "The Development of the Tourist Industry in Barbados," in DeLisle Worrell (ed.), *The Economy of Barbados, 1946–1980*, p. 117.

15. Central Bank of Barbados, *Annual Statistical Digest, 1992* (Barbados: The Central Bank of Barbados, 1992), Table J3, p. 203, and J4, p. 204.

16. Calculated from The World Bank, *World Tables 1993* (Washington, DC: The World Bank, 1993), p. 116.

17. The index of production of electronic components (1982 = 100) fell from 136.1 in 1986 to 44.6 in 1987 and stayed at approximately that level throughout the remainder of the period. See Central Bank of Barbados, *Annual Statistical Digest, 1992*, Table I5, pp. 180–181.

18. Calculated from ibid., Table H12, pp. 170–171.

19. See Central Bank of Barbados, *Annual Report, 1991* (Barbados: The Central Bank of Barbados, 1991), p. 3.

20. The World Bank, *St. Christopher and Nevis: Economic Report* (Washington, DC: The World Bank, 1985), p. 13.

21. Ibid., p.14.

22. Carleen O'Loughlin, *Economic and Political Change in the Leeward and Windward Islands* (New Haven: Yale University Press, 1968), pp. 105–106.

23. Michel-Rolph Trouillot, *Peasants and Capital; Dominica in the World Economy* (Baltimore: The Johns Hopkins University Press, 1988), pp. 148, 157.

24. Latin America Bureau, *Green Gold: Bananas and Dependency in the Eastern Caribbean* (London: Latin America Bureau, 1987), pp. 10–11.

25. The World Bank, *St. Lucia: Economic Performance and Prospects* (Washington, DC: The World Bank, 1985), p. 21.

26. Ibid., p. 24.

27. Sidney E. Chernick, *The Commonwealth Caribbean*, p. 149.

28. Ibid., pp. 149–150.

29. Jost Krippendorf, *The Holiday Makers: Understanding the Impact of Leisure and Travel* (Oxford: Butterworth Heinemann, 1992), pp. 48, 122.

30. Auliana Poon, "Caribbean Tourism and the World Economy," in Stanley Lalta and Marie Freckleton (eds.), *Caribbean Economic Development: The First Generation*, pp. 262–263.

31. Ibid., pp. 267, 268.

32. Ibid., p. 272.

33. Ibid., pp. 279, 273.

34. Ibid., p. 272.

35. Jost Krippendorf, *The Holiday Makers*, p. 74.

CHAPTER 8

Exports and Education

As noted in Chapter 5, William G. Demas, then head of the Economic Planning Division of Trinidad and Tobago, in a series of lectures delivered at McGill University in 1964, argued that small open economies such as those in the Caribbean, "can achieve transformation only on the basis of developing exports of manufactured goods." Demas believed that the opportunity for the region to export raw materials and agricultural goods was limited. Further he pointed to constraints on production for the domestic market because of "the lack of a diversified resource base and the absence of opportunities for economies of scale in industrial programmes devoted to the home market alone." With "exporting manufactures being more difficult than producing them for the home market," Demas urged an immediate shift to an export orientation since "the earlier the learning process starts the better."[1]

Thirty years later, another Trinidad economist gave witness to the region's failure to follow Demas' strictures. Writing in the early 1990s, Trevor Farrell reported that the region was "stuck with a set of export specializations most of which have lost their growth dynamic, have become subject to steadily increasing competition from new suppliers, and/or from substitutes," and where, in consequence, "relative prices, profits, availability of capital for investment and net contribution to the balance of payments, government revenue etc. have all tended or are tending, to deteriorate." The problem was that over this thirty year period no change had occurred in the structure of the region's exports. As a result, the West Indies had persisted in producing for markets which had long since peaked in their income-generating capacity. As

151

Table 1

Caribbean Countries Grouped by Average Annual Percent Growth of GDP, 1981–90

	Growth rate	Population
Small nations		
Antigua and Barbuda	6.3	79,000
Dominica	4.4	72,000
Grenada	4.7	91,000
St. Kitts and Nevis	5.1	40,000
St. Lucia	4.5	150,000
St. Vincent and the Grenadines	6.4	107,000
Total	5.2[1]	539,000
Larger nations		
Barbados	0.8	257,000
Jamaica	1.8	2,356,000
Trinidad and Tobago	−2.6	1,236,000
Guyana	−2.8	798,000
Total	−0.2[1]	4,647,000
Entire West Indies		
Total	0.3[1]	5,186,000

[1]Population-weighted growth rate.

Sources: Growth rates: Computed from The World Bank, *Caribbean Region: Current Economic Situation, Regional Issues and Capital Flows, 1992,* Table 1.2, p. 136; Population: The World Bank, *World Tables, 1993* (Washington. DC: The World Bank, 1993).

Farrell puts it, in the 1990s "all of the key export sectors of the region are in deep trouble — sugar, bauxite, oil, bananas and tourism."[2]

This failure dramatically to expand and change the composition of exports resulted, during the 1980s, in an unsatisfactory economic growth experience. It is true, as indicated in Table 1, that six countries, Antigua and Barbuda, Dominica, Grenada, St. Kitts and Nevis, St. Lucia, and St. Vincent

Table 2

U.S. Imports from Caribbean Basin Initiative Designated Countries, 1985–92 (US$ 000)

Country	1985	1992	% change
West Indies excluding Trinidad and Tobago	564,594[1]	788,132[2]	+39.6
Trinidad and Tobago	1,255,498	839,787	–33.1
All West Indies	1,820,092[1]	1,627,919[2]	–10.6
Central America	2,095,344	3,983,972	+90.1
All Countries[3]	4,012,482	9,425,616	+134.9

[1]Guyana not included since it was not a designated country under the CBER.
[2]Guyana included. [3]Non–oil-producing countries.

Source: United States International Trade Commission, *Annual Report on the Impact of the Caribbean Basin Economic Recovery Act on U.S. Industries and Consumers, Fifth Report, 1989 (September 1990) and Eighth Report, 1992 (September 1993)*, Table 2-2.

and the Grenadines experienced very high rates of expansion. The combined population of these countries, however, was only 539,000. In contrast, over 2 million people were resident in Guyana and Trinidad and Tobago where, over the decade, a serious economic decline was experienced. A further 2.6 million lived in Jamaica and Barbados where something close to economic stagnation occurred. Thus only 10 percent of the region's population lived in nations of expansion. The remaining 90 percent resided where either negative growth or at best stagnation was experienced.

Another dimension of this failure is made clear in Table 2. That table compares the response of the West Indies and that of Central America and the rest of South American to the United States' Caribbean Basin Initiative (CBI). For designated countries, the CBI reduced or eliminated United States tariffs for a wide variety of goods, though it did exclude certain products important to the West Indies such as sugar, petroleum and textiles. Nonetheless, CBI made access to the United States market much easier. The response to the CBI thus acts as an indicator of the relative ability of the region to take advantage of new market opportunities.

The West Indies' capacity to take advantage of this increased opportunity to export was relatively poor. Excluding Trinidad and Tobago from the regional experience eliminates the distorting effects of that country's diminished petroleum sales to the United States. By excluding Trinidad and Tobago, a 10 percent decline in regional exports to the United States turns into a nearly 40 percent increase. Even so, however, that 40 percent increase in exports to the United States over the seven year period compares unfavorably with the 90 percent growth which occurred in Central American and the more than doubling which was experienced among all CBI designated countries taken together. The West Indies did respond to the CBI, but its response was sluggish compared to other comparably situated countries.

The failure substantially to increase export earnings was fundamental to the balance of payments crisis which was experienced by Barbados, Guyana, Jamaica, and Trinidad and Tobago in this period. What happened in each case was that declining export earnings were not matched by comparable reductions in imports. Capital inflows were insufficient to finance the imbalance between the two. As a result, each fell into arrears with regard to debt service as well as to the repayment of loans. Invariably, a resolution to that crisis involved securing financing from World Bank and/or the International Monetary Fund. But the securing of such assistance necessitated agreement to conditions imposed by those multilateral institutions. Those conditions were always the same. They required a "structural adjustment," the goal of which was "reducing the size and scope of the public sector, and stimulating investment and growth through the development of an efficient private sector." The hope was that in doing so the countries would be "well positioned to augment their shares in the tourism market and to penetrate extra-regional markets."[3] The Bank claimed that the policy changes it insisted upon would be the means by which to increase exports.

According to the IMF and World Bank, exports lag because the wrong policies are followed. In this view prices are the key to exports, and if a country is not exporting adequately it is because the government's policies are resulting in uncompetitively high prices. Such high prices result, in this view, from what it calls an inward-oriented trade strategy. High import tariffs, import quotas or overvalued exchange rates all tend to result in uncompetitively high prices for a country's output. Tariffs and quotas raise the price of imported inputs compared to the price which would be paid in their absence and thereby inflate costs. An excessively high exchange rate inflates the price of exports to consumers on world markets. In addition, protection in general is viewed negatively since it spares domestic producers the necessity of competing with cost-minimizing overseas producers. In general, argues the World Bank, "the advantage of an outward-oriented strategy over an inward-oriented strategy is that it promotes the efficient use of resources."[4]

Enhanced competitiveness in this view is associated with private commercial investment. Public ownership of businesses harms exports because in such enterprises "short-term political objectives can override concerns for long-term economic viability."[5] But so too does government spending and taxes. These drain the pool of resources available for private investment. To be sure, the Bank acknowledges the need for government spending on infrastructure and education. Governments are successful in promoting growth, the Bank argues, when "they have established clear rules of the game, contributed judiciously to the construction of an industrial infrastructure, and otherwise intervened sparingly and carefully." The Bank warns that "some developing countries however, have undermined their industrialization efforts by approaching these choices in reverse."[6]

When the World Bank provides loans to a country it insists, in return, on its "reform agenda." In the Caribbean, as elsewhere, what is called for is a reduction in the size of Government, a lowering of tariffs, depreciation of the local currency, and the privatizing of public sector commercial enterprises. The Bank believes that governments in the region both tax and spend too much, employ too many individuals and pay excessively high wage rates. It requires extensive privatization, arguing that in doing so governments will be able to specialize in the activities which they are best equipped to perform, the providing of public goods like infrastructure.[7] The Bank believes that "combinations of currency depreciation and trade policies will improve the region's competitiveness" and that a number of countries require "a more competitive and attractive real exchange rate than that achieved in the past" if they are to achieve a higher level of exports.[8] Finally, it calls for a reduction in tariff protection. It does recognize that when the West Indies countries in the Caribbean Community (CARICOM) approved a new Common External Tariff (CET) in October 1992 the region moved substantially in that direction. Even so, the bank stated that it would like to see a "rapid implementation of the new CET" at a quicker pace than the 4–5 year period envisioned by CARICOM.[9] In general, the Bank's recommendations for the region are simply a specific application of its general prescription for enhancing competitiveness. Exposure to international competition, currency depreciation, a reduced claim to social resources by the government, and in particular, excluding government from commercial activities, are what, for the World Bank and the IMF represent an appropriate strategy of growth.

The worry in all of this is that the World Bank's analysis of the Caribbean's problems may be inadequate. It is possible that the difficulties which constrain the region's development may not be amenable to solution by the strategies suggested by this official source. Making more resources available to local business and increasing its exposure to competition, and reducing export prices by devaluing the currency may not be all that is required for the region to achieve successes in export markets. The hypothesis which must be considered is that in a context of economic liberalism, West Indian businesses may simply be overwhelmed by competition from abroad. They may not be now nor in the foreseeable future equipped successfully to meet the challenge of international competition. If that is the case, opening the economy would not solve the problem, but rather would expose the region to even more difficulties that currently are experienced.

This is essentially the message that the University of the West Indies economist, Trevor Farrell, delivers. For Farrell finds the weaknesses of the Caribbean export performance not solely or even primarily in the economic sphere. Exports fail, in his analysis, because the fundamentals of export marketing are not understood and recognized. It is not the lack of resources which constrains the region in this regard, but rather educational and other non-economic institutions which result in "the failure to develop people with a capacity and willingness to think things through for themselves and engage in creative problem solving."[10] Farrell believes that it is possible for a small region like the Caribbean to identify and exploit market opportunities made possible by technological change. The Caribbean could have taken advantage of the introduction of the video cassette recorder by becoming a major supplier of recorded material, or it could have seized the opportunities created by the introduction of personal computers to become a producer of peripherals and software. While those possibilities are long gone, he nonetheless believes that opportunities continuously are being created. What the region must do is learn to "rid[e] the coattails of the axial product."[11]

But to do that, the region must increase its ability to anticipate opportunities much more than is presently the case. In Farrell's words, it must develop the capacity to respond speedily and possess a "highly developed cerebral apparatus." And that is where the Bank's diagnosis and policy recommendations are inadequate. For what Farrell thinks is that successful participation in export markets imposes "a set of sociological requirements" which the region has not satisfied and which the World Bank does not address. Foremost among the many changes which would be needed are those relating to the education of the West Indian people. Farrell writes that "wide-ranging educational reform would undoubtedly be required both in terms of curricu-

Table 3

Index of Dollar Exchange Rate with United States, Government Consumption as Percent of Gross Domestic Product at Market Prices and Merchandise Exports in December 1981 US Dollars, Jamaica, 1971/75–1986/90

	Exchange rate 1971–75 = 100	Government consumption as % of GDP	Merchandise exports in 1981 US$
1971–75	100	15.7	1072.9
1976–80	66	20.2	1155.8
1981–85	32	18.9	755.3
1986–90	14	14.8	720.1

Sources: Exchange Rate, Government Consumption as Percent of GDP, and Merchandise Trade Computed from *The World Bank, World Tables 1993* (Washington, DC: The World Bank, 1993), pp. 346–347; Merchandise Trade: *The World Bank, World Tables 1993*, pp. 346–347, and Merchandise Trade deflated by Consumer Price Index CPI-U-X1, *Economic Report of the President 1994* (Washington, DC: Government Printing Office, 1994), Table B-61, p. 338.

lum content and the approach to education and ... training and re-training would have to become really big business."[12]

One test of the adequacy of the World Bank/IMF strategy for the Caribbean is to examine the recent experience of Jamaica. That country has been under the influence of IMF conditionalities since the late 1970s. Whereas it might be argued that the implementation of the IMF/World Bank approach elsewhere in the region is too recent to provide a fair assessment of its efficacy, that is not the case with Jamaica. Indeed, with regard to the most important variables emphasized by the World Bank, the exchange rate and the relative size of government, Table 3 shows that Jamaica to a large extent has done what has been asked of it. There has been a massive depreciation in the value of the Jamaica dollar. The reduction in government consumption as a percentage of Gross Domestic Product is less dramatic, but yet remains significant. The Government share of GDP actually peaked at 22.0 percent in 1982. Thereafter it steadily declined so that by the end of the period the share had fallen back to the level it had last attained in 1972.

But what the table also makes clear is that these two adjustments were not adequate to allow Jamaica to become a successful exporter. The merchandise exports which are reported in Table 3 are in U.S. dollars adjusted for inflation in that country. What, in effect, they represent is the level of purchases from the United States which Jamaican exports permitted. As is clear the experience has not been a successful one. Merchandise exports expressed in this way were 37.7 percent lower in 1986/90 than they had been ten years earlier. Of course it could be argued that this trend would have been more favorable if Jamaica had not only devalued its currency and reduced the role of government, but had also exposed itself more to international competition by lowering its tariffs. This may be the case, though the data presented here do not point in that direction. Instead they seem to support Farrell's view that for the region to become successful in overseas markets involves more fundamental changes than those suggested by the World Bank and the IMF. Even though the kind of structural adjustments advocated by the multilateral lending agencies were to a considerable extent implemented, there obviously were other obstacles than these which prevented Jamaica from becoming a success as an exporter of manufactured goods.[13] With this the case for Jamaica, and in light of their similar economic histories and structure, it would seem likely that other countries in the region such as Barbados, Guyana, and Trinidad and Tobago will experience the same frustration with the World Bank/IMF reforms. Farrell, in short, seems to be right. The problem of export promotion, and therefore, economic development in the Caribbean, requires a consideration of other variables than those relating to prices and the role of government. The basis of productive competence must be considered. Fundamental here is the fact that familiarity with modern technology is essential for success in world markets. That familiarity is available only to a population which possesses a high level of scientific and engineering education.

It is in this perspective that it is possible to understand how the history and the structure of the societies of the Commonwealth Caribbean conspire against the process of economic modernization. Under slavery all formal education was denied to virtually the entire population. But even after Emancipation this anti-education bias continued. With the persistence of non slave plantation agriculture, the region's employers maintained their pattern of hiring large numbers of unskilled workers. Education for the bulk of society was viewed by the planters and their political allies as unnecessary and undesirable. Thus it was that the territories of the region became independent nations with market economies, but were able to secure only very limited innovation in production. Based on this history, the people of the

Table 4

Percentage Increase in Real Gross Domestic Product, Selected Asian Countries, 1980–89

Country	Percentage increase	Population
Hong Kong	84.7	5,761,000
Korea	122.9	42,380,000
Malaysia	62.6	17,353,000
Mauritius	68.4	1,062,000
Singapore	82.3	2,952,000
Thailand	92.4	55,448,000
Turkey	54.1	51,233,900
Unweighted mean	81.1	
Population weighted mean	84.3	

Source: *The World Bank, World Tables 1993* (Washington, DC: The World Bank, 1993).

Caribbean, both workers and managers alike, lack, in the contemporary period, the technical competence to create an modern economy.

There is a paradox in pointing to education as a weakness in Caribbean efforts to achieve economic modernization. For as Franklin W. Knight has pointed out, in the Caribbean "public education is recognized as a great lever for upward social and economic mobility." Even so, as Knight himself underlines, at the tertiary level of education the region is quite weak.[14] The problem with this is that increasingly, as technology advances, it is a university education which is essential for technical competence.

In order to provide perspective on the Caribbean, it is useful to compare it with exporting-oriented, Asian countries. The population-weighted growth of selected Asian countries in the 1980s was 84.3 percent (Table 4). By contrast, the population weighted growth for the Caribbean was 1.1 percent (Table 5). The hypothesis which suggests itself is that the group of Asian countries enjoyed a much more rapid rate of economic expansion than occurred in the Caribbean because the citizens of those countries were better

Table 5

Percentage Increase in Gross Domestic Product, Caribbean Countries, 1980–89

Country	Percentage increase	Population
Antigua and Barbuda	77.0	79,000
Barbados	19.4	257,000
Dominica	58.4	73,000
Grenada	NA	
Guyana	–24.1	796,000
Jamaica	16.6	2,339,000
St. Kitts and Nevis	55.4	41,000
St. Lucia	NA	
St. Vincent and the Grenadines	79.3	106,000
Trinidad and Tobago	–32.9	1,221,000
Unweighted mean	31.1	
Population weighted mean	1.1	

Source: See Table 4.

educated and possessed to a greater extent the human capital necessary to introduce and work efficiently in a technically advanced environment.

Table 6 compares several measures of higher education in the Caribbean with those for the Asian countries. The pattern is unmistakable. In every measure reported, the Caribbean lags seriously behind the Asian countries. The latter have four times as many scientists and technicians per 1000 of the population, two and a half times as many research and development workers, more than twice the rate of tertiary graduates, almost twice the tertiary enrollment rate, and spends more than twice the share of public expenditures on higher education than do the Caribbean countries.

What makes these results significant is that with the exception of Hong Kong and Singapore, the Asian countries included in our comparison are not remarkably wealthy. It is true that the per capita income in Hong Kong and

Table 6

Selected Measures of Human Capital Appropriate for Technological Advance, Commonwealth Caribbean* and Selected Asian Countries,* 1985–90

	Caribbean	Asian
Scientists and technicians per 1000 population	6.7[1]	26.1[2]
Research and development scientists and technicians per 1000 population	2.5[3]	6.7[4]
Tertiary graduates as % of age group	1.4[3]	3.2[5]
Tertiary enrollment rate	8.5[6]	15.0
Higher education as % of all public expenditures	7.0[7]	16.1[8]

*Caribbean: Barbados, Trinidad and Tobago, Dominica, Antigua and Barbuda, Grenada, Jamaica, St. Lucia, St. Vincent and the Grenadines, St. Kitts and Nevis, and Guyana. Asia: Hong Kong, Mauritius, Malaysia, Thailand, Turkey, Korea, and Singapore.

[1]Barbados, Guyana, Jamaica. [2]Hong Kong, Mauritius, Thailand, Turkey, Korea, Singapore. [3]Guyana, Jamaica, Trinidad and Tobago. [4]No data for Hong Kong and Singapore. [5]No data for Korea and Singapore. [6]Barbados, Trinidad and Tobago, Jamaica, Guyana. [7]Barbados, Trinidad and Tobago, Jamaica, Grenada, St. Lucia, St. Vincent and the Grenadines, St. Kitts and Nevis. [8]No data for Hong Kong.

Source: Calculated from United Nations Development Programme, *Human Development Report, 1992* (New York: Oxford University Press, 1992), Table 5, p. 136; Table 14, p. 154; Table 15, p. 156.

Singapore was greater than $(US) 11,000, far exceeding that of any country in the region. However, Barbados' per capita income of $(US) 6,540 was greater than that of the Republic of Korea where the level was $(US) 5,400; and Thailand, Malaysia, Mauritius and Turkey, with per capita incomes ranging between $(US) 1,420 and $(US) 2,320, were roughly similar to most of the countries of the Caribbean.[15] Thus tertiary school performance cannot be considered as a luxury the Asian countries can indulge in because of their wealth. Rather, what unites these countries is their rapid growth rate. The fact is that at levels of income comparable to those in the Caribbean, the Asian countries are much more committed to higher education and especially to the training of scientists and engineers. This commitment is clearly one of the factors which contributes to their rapid economic growth compared to the Caribbean.

In discussing the relevance of the Asian growth experience to the Caribbean, the economist Winston H. Griffith takes note of the importance of education. Griffith writes that "to ensure that they have the personnel to compete in a high-tech world, East Asian countries have been spending large sums of money on technical education." In contrast, he notes that the Caribbean is "short of the skills required to develop the new technology." In this regard he cites a *Wall Street Journal* report concerning the closing of the electronics facility in Barbados mentioned in Chapter 7. The manager of the plant was quoted as saying that contributing to the decision to close was the fact that it "was unlikely to find a dozen electrical engineers in Barbados." Griffith concludes that it is "pointless for Caribbean governments to talk about attracting high-technology firms when they are reluctant, for whatever reasons, to give the University of the West Indies the resources to restructure an educational system."[16] In confirmation of the thesis of inadequate tertiary education in the Caribbean, Knight cites data provided in 1989 by the University of the West Indies which shows that about 12,000 students attended that institution's three campuses in that year. By way of contrast, Knight writes that "Puerto Rico, with just about the same population ... had more than 200,000 students enrolled at the university level."[17]

Though these data might be interpreted as suggesting that the problem with education in the West Indies resides exclusively at the tertiary level, that does not appear to be the case. Rather the educational bottleneck appears far earlier, at the primary and secondary school levels.

In the first place, for many students the quality of the education they receive is less than adequate. The reason for this is insufficient teacher training. Such training in the region is supposed to occur either in two years of course work or in an in-service program. The problem is that a high proportion of teachers in the region lack such training. Among the OECS countries, as reported in Table 7, Antigua has the highest proportion of trained teachers, but even there 26 percent of primary school teachers lacked such preparation. This statistic is highest in St. Vincent and the Grenadines where in 1990, 72 percent of teachers lacked full qualifications to teach. What is worse, in five of the six countries listed in the table, the proportion of trained teachers declined between the mid-1980s and 1990.

Table 7

Proportion of Trained Primary School
Teachers, 1984–87, 1990

Country	1984–87	1990
Antigua	80	74
Dominica	44	43
Grenada	47	39
St. Kitts	72	64
St. Lucia	53	61
St. Vincent	36	28

Source: The World Bank, *Caribbean Region: Access, Quality and Efficiency in Education* (Washington, DC: The World Bank, 1993), Table 4.

The result of the deficiency in teacher training is predictable. The World Bank's report on education in the region contains a catalogue of problems. In Jamaica, 31 percent of primary school graduates are functionally illiterate; the overall standard of mathematics in Dominica is reported to be "low"; similarly, in Guyana "the effectiveness of schooling appears to be similarly low"; and even in Barbados, the country with the most effective educational system in the region, it is reported that "there had been a deterioration in reading achievement." The Bank concludes its country by country assessment by declaring that, though quantitative data on the subject are scarce, those data that have been produced "suggest that quality is low throughout the Region, particularly in the areas of reading, writing and numeracy."[18]

In addition to the problems of educational quality, there are simply too few secondary school spaces available for Caribbean students. Table 8 presents data on the probabilities of entering or completing threshold levels of education in the region. The most favorable dimension of the patterns observed in this table is that access to primary schooling is virtually universal. Furthermore, everywhere a high proportion of students completes that level of formal education. But in most countries there is a devastating step down between the percentage of children who complete primary school and those who enter secondary schools. In Dominica, Guyana and St. Lucia the

Table 8

Probabilities of Different Levels of Educational Attainment[1]

Country	Enter primary	Complete primary	Enter secondary	Complete secondary	Enter tertiary and univ.
Antigua	100	98	55	NA	1.50[2]
Barbados	100	100	96	NA	45.00
Dominica	100	93	25	NA	3.25
Grenada	100	95	45	38	1.00
Guyana	100	80	26	26	2.00
Jamaica	100	85	53	53	2.00
St. Kitts	100	97	93	NA	2.00
St. Lucia	100	93	23	21	1.00
St. Vincent	100	98	39	NA	0.50
Trinidad	100	100	70	65	3.00

[1]Probabilities based on each 100 primary school entrants. [2]Tertiary not available.

Source: The World Bank, *Caribbean Region: Access, Quality and Efficiency in Education* (Washington, DC: The World Bank, 1993,), Table 3.1, p. 45.

situation is disastrous. Only about one in four children enters secondary school in those countries. This percentage is not much better in Antigua, Grenada and Jamaica where the corresponding statistic is approximately one in two. Even Trinidad and Tobago, a relatively wealthy and well-educated nation by Caribbean standards, sees 30 percent of its children fail to enter a secondary school. Only Barbados and St. Kitts provide secondary school enrollment for virtually all of their primary school leavers.

In principle it is possible that this drastic decline in school attendance at the secondary school level reflects the choice of the Caribbean people to cut short their formal education and voluntarily leave school at the primary level. But almost certainly that is not the case. Entry into secondary school in the Caribbean is allotted on the basis of student performance in the examination which is administered near the end of the primary school experience. Many more students take this examination than pass it. The low pass rate reflects the use of the examination's grades as a rationing device. Those grades rank order student test takers. A cutoff grade is set at the level at which the number

Table 9

**Probability of Entering Secondary School as
Percentage of Probability of Completing Primary
School and Probability of Entering Tertiary
School Percentage of Probability of
Completing Secondary School**

	% accommodated at secondary level	% accommodated at tertiary level
Antigua	56.1	NA
Barbados	96.0	NA
Dominica	26.9	NA
Grenada	47.4	2.6
Guyana	32.5	7.7
Jamaica	62.4	3.8
St. Kitts	95.9	NA
St. Lucia	24.7	4.8
St. Vincent	39.8	NA
Trinidad	70.0	4.6

Source: Computed from Table 8.

of students matches the available space in the secondary schools of the individual countries. Thus the sharp decline in school attendance which occurs at the secondary school level almost certainly reflects a lack of opportunity rather than the preference of Caribbean children and their parents.[19]

Data dealing with the ratio of primary school students seeking to attend secondary school relative to the availability of such places do not seem to exist. In their absence the availability of secondary school spaces can only be inferred. Such inferences can be made from the data in Table 7. If it were assumed that all primary school graduates wished to attend secondary school, then the percentage of students who enter secondary school divided by the percentage who complete primary school would provide an estimate of the proportion of students who can be accommodated at that higher level.

Those percentages are provided in Table 9. They indicate that while Barbados and St. Kitts have provided secondary school opportunities for virtually all of their primary school graduates, the experience is much less satisfactory elsewhere. In this interpretation less than one-half of primary school leavers have the opportunity to go to secondary school in St. Lucia, Dominica, Guyana, St. Vincent, and Grenada. Jamaica and Trinidad do better but even in those countries attrition is imposed on at least 30 percent of primary school graduates.

It is of course likely that not all primary school graduates in the Caribbean wish to attend secondary school. To the extent that this is so, these estimates of the percentage of students who are denied the opportunity to continue their education is inflated. The fact however, that in both St. Kitts and Barbados the percentage of primary school completers who enter secondary school is about 96 percent, suggests that the distortion associated with this procedure is not large. Certainly the overwhelming likelihood is that if new places were opened at the secondary school level, they would be filled by students who are shut out from this educational opportunity.

Performing the same calculations for the transition between secondary and tertiary education suggests that the bottleneck at this level is even more severe than between primary and secondary schools. Only limited data are available on this and coverage is confined to five countries. In particular the omission of Barbados, where there is an extensive tertiary level educational system, biases the results in a downward direction. Nevertheless, the low probability of entering a tertiary institution is striking. Among the five countries for which data are available, Guyana does best, but even there only 7.7 percent of secondary graduates can look forward to a university or other tertiary level education.

What all of this suggests is that the educational system in the West Indies acts as an important brake on the region's economic modernization efforts. Both the qualitative and quantitative deficiencies of the region's educational system result in the West Indies' labor force not possessing the level of academic achievement that effective participation in technologically sophisticated world markets requires. Only in Barbados has half of the working age population completed a secondary school education. In Trinidad and Tobago that statistic is only about one-third. But elsewhere the share of secondary school graduates stands at only about one-fifth of the population (Table 10).

That level of education simply does not equip the region's population with the analytic and communications skills which modern technology requires. The World Bank's report on education in the region, in short, has good reason to argue that "until the primary schools can significantly improve the performance level of their graduates and secondary schools and tertiary institu-

Table 10

Percent Distribution of Population of Working Age by Education Attainment, 1980–81

| Country | Level of education[1] | | |
	None, nursery and primary	Secondary	University
Antigua	NA	NA	NA
Barbados	42.4	50.7	3.7
Dominica	81.1	16.2	1.7
Grenada	76.3	20.4	1.9
Guyana	71.8	23.9	1.4
Jamaica	NA	NA	NA
St. Kitts	NA	NA	NA
St. Lucia	80.2	17.7	1.0
St. Vincent	78.7	19.2	0.9
Trinidad	61.9	35.5	2.4

[1]Numbers may not add up to 100% due to exclusion of "other" category.

Source: The World Bank, *Caribbean Region: Access, Quality and Efficiency in Education* (Washington, DC: The World Bank, 1993), Table A-6, p. 241.

tions offer a sound education for a much larger proportion of the age group than is currently the case, it is unlikely that most Caribbean nations' labor force will be capable of supporting a development strategy dependent more on human than natural resources."[20]

It is because of these circumstances that migration from the region has been especially damaging. Emigration is a process which involves the self-selection of individuals who judge that by relocating they will be able to improve their economic well-being. Those most likely to make this judgment are the people of the Caribbean who possess the kind and quality of education increasingly in demand in the United States labor market. As we have seen, West Indians have never been reluctant to employ mobility as a means to secure a higher standard of living. So it is now. As Ralph Henry has put it, "those with higher levels of education and training, which afford them a greater probability of securing immigrant visas to the United States and Canada," are the people most likely to emigrate.[21]

Table 11

Emigration to the United States by Country, 1980–88

Country	Total emigration	Emigration as % of population
Antigua	11576	14.5
Barbados	16788	7.2
Dominica	5579	7.2
Grenada	9437	9.8
Guyana	81604	10.3
Jamaica	183239	7.8
St. Kitts	9792	22.3
St. Lucia	5761	4.2
St. Vincent	6451	5.5
Trinidad	32553	2.7
Total	372572	7.5

Source: The World Bank, *Caribbean Region: Access, Quality and Efficiency in Education* (Washington, DC: The World Bank, 1993), Table 1.8, p. 11.

Recent migration has been very high indeed. Table 11 provides information on migration to the United States between 1980 and 1988. In those years the Caribbean annually lost almost 1 percent (actually 0.94 percent) of its population in this way. About one half of this migration came from Jamaica, and another one-fifth came from Guyana. The region's highest rates of out migration however were experienced in St. Kitts where almost 10,000 people left this country of about 44,000, and Antigua where 14.5 percent of the population left the island.

But it is not merely the number of emigres from the West Indies which is important. The migration has also seriously depleted the quality of the labor force resident in the region. The outward flow of people is disproportionately composed of relatively well-educated individuals, precisely the category which, as we have seen, the region's educational system has failed to produce in adequate numbers. Data in this regard are scarce but what are available are consistent. Reports from Jamaica, Grenada, and Trinidad and Tobago all attest to the fact that the emigration of professional, technical and skilled workers is high. Averille White's study of Eastern Caribbean migrants in the United States indicates that more than 50 percent of arrivals from the Eastern Caribbean possessed at least four years of high school and that 13.9 percent of males and 6.5 percent of females completed four or more years of college.[22] Such relatively well-educated workers are at least twice as heavily represented in the outflow from the region as they are present in the Caribbean's labor force. Henry's judgement is that "where Caribbean economies and their governments fail the test of providing what is regarded as a decent standard of living ... their skilled, professional and trained people ... exercise the option of voting with their feet."[23]

The migration therefore complicates an already difficult situation. As things stand at present, the countries of the region do not adequately educate their populations to participate effectively in the modern world economy. In addition, a large proportion of those who are educated leave the region. Emigration, therefore, means that in order to increase the quality of the Caribbean labor force, substantial inefficiencies will be confronted. Many more students will have to be educated through secondary school than there will be additions of well-educated individuals to the labor force. The migration means, in the words of a World Bank report, "that many countries are not reaping the full benefits of their social investment in education."[24] Migration makes advances in the quality of the regional labor force, as measured by an increased proportion of secondary school graduates, more expensive than it would be if the population were less mobile.

But while migration has made education more expensive, in most of the countries of the region recurrent educational outlays as a percentage of gross domestic product have declined (Table 12). Such a fall occurred in six of the nine countries for which adequate data are available. In Trinidad and Tobago there was an increase in the ratio of educational expenditures to GDP, but since it occurred while the country's GDP was declining precipitously there, educational expenditures declined in absolute terms. Capital expenditures in education may have fared even worse than recurrent expenses. Since firm data are available for only Barbados, Jamaica, and Trinidad and Tobago, generalizations for the whole region are risky. Nonetheless in each of these countries, capital expenditures in education as a share of total government investment declined markedly: from 19.0 to 3.6 percent in Barbados; from 4.3 to 3.0 in Trinidad and Tobago; and from 4.3 to 1.3 in Jamaica over the period between 1982 and 1987.[25] What seems likely is that the fiscal austerity which indebtedness imposed on the public sector in the region did not spare educational outlays. Just at the time that the cost of augmenting the level of educational attainment of the labor force was going up, educational expenditures fell.

Table 12

**Recurrent Government Education Expenditure
as a Share of GNP, 1984, 1988**

Country	1984	1988	Change
Antigua	2.5	2.4	−0.1
Barbados	5.5	5.4	−0.1
Dominica	5.7	4.9	−0.8
Grenada	6.4	4.6	−1.8
Guyana	NA	2.9	NA
Jamaica	5.2	4.8	−0.4
St. Kitts	4.1	3.5	−0.6
St. Lucia	7.2	8.6	+1.4
St. Vincent	5.9	6.1	+0.2
Trinidad	5.1	5.6	+0.5

Source: The World Bank, *Caribbean Region: Access, Quality and Efficiency in Education* (Washington, DC: The World Bank, 1993), Table 2.2, p. 25.

It may be possible to reverse the downward trend in recurrent expenditures. The World Bank suggests that as the structural adjustment which it recommends is implemented, resources will be freed up which could be used in educational outlays. But the Bank also urges that capital investment in education be increased. In this regard it recommends looking for external sources of support. Indeed there does not seem to be much doubt that if large increments in expenditures are going to be made in education it will be only if external financing can be found.[26]

Yet the results of these efforts are likely to be inadequate. Raising expenditures sufficiently to provide secondary school education for a far higher proportion of Caribbean children than receive it to date will prove to be an expensive project. This is because educational outlays cannot discriminate between those who will stay in the region and the relatively high number of people who will emigrate. To educate enough children both to compensate for the emigration, and still significantly increase the secondary graduation rates present in the remaining labor force, is to ask much. The nations of the

Caribbean already spend a higher share of their Gross Domestic Product on education than is the case in any other region of the developing world.[27] The simple fact is that the heavy loss of educated individuals from the region makes West Indies educational expenditures relatively inefficient in producing advances in the quality of the regional labor force.

NOTES

1. William G. Demas, *The Economics of Development in Small Countries with Special Reference to the Caribbean*, pp. 132–133.

2. Trevor Farrell, "Some Notes Towards a Strategy For Economic Transformation," in Stanley Lalta and Marie Freckleton (eds.), *Caribbean Economic Development: The First Generation*, pp. 333, 331.

3. The World Bank, *Caribbean Region: Current Economic Situation, Regional Issues and Capital Flows, 1992*, p. 13.

4. The World Bank, *World Development Report 1987* (Washington, DC: Oxford University Press, 1987), p. 90.

5. The World Bank, *Caribbean Region: Current Economic Situation, Regional Issues and Capital Flows, 1992*, p. 15.

6. The World Bank, *World Development Report, 1987*, p. 60.

7. The World Bank, *Caribbean Region: Current Economic Situation, Regional Issues and Capital Flows, 1992*, pp. 11–14.

8. Ibid., p. 13.

9. Ibid., p. 23.

10. Trevor M.A. Farrell, "Some Notes Towards a Strategy for Economic Transformation," in Stanley Lalta and Marie Freckleton (eds.), *Caribbean Economic Development: The First Generation*, p. 335.

11. Ibid., pp. 338–339.

12. Ibid., pp. 340, 341.

13. See Janine Iqbal, "Adjustment Policies in Practice: Case Study of Jamaica 1977–91," in Stanley Lalta and Marie Freckleton (eds.), *Caribbean Economic Development: The First Generation*, pp. 47–67.

14. Franklin W. Knight, "The Societies of the Caribbean since Independence," in Jorge I. Dominguez, Robert A. Pastor, and R. DeLisle Worrell (eds.), *Democracy in the Caribbean: Political, Economic and Social Perspectives* (Baltimore: The Johns Hopkins University Press, 1993), p. 36.

15. The World Bank, *World Tables, 1992* (Baltimore: The Johns Hopkins University Press, 1992).

16. Winston H. Griffith, "The Applicability of the East Asian Experience to Caribbean Countries," in Yin-Kann Wen and Jayshree Sengupta (eds.), *Increasing*

the *International Competitiveness of Exports from Caribbean Countries* (Washington, DC: The World Bank, 1991), pp. 96–97.

17. Franklin W. Knight, "The Societies of the Caribbean since Independence," in Jorge I. Dominguez, Robert A. Pastor, and R. DeLisle Worrell (eds.), *Democracy in the Caribbean*, p. 36.

18. The World Bank, *Caribbean Region: Access, Quality, and Efficiency in Education* (Washington, DC: The World Bank, 1993), pp. 65, 63, 64, 63, 68.

19. Ibid., p. 62.

20. The World Bank, *Caribbean Region: Access, Quality and Efficiency in Education*, p. 44.

21. Ralph M. Henry, "A Reinterpretation of Labor Services of the Commonwealth Caribbean," in Anthony P. Maingot (ed.), *Small Country Development and International Labor Flows: Experiences in the Caribbean* (Boulder: Westview Press, 1991), p. 120.

22. Computed from Averille White, "Eastern Caribbean Migrants in the U.S.A.: A Demographic Profile," *Bulletin of Eastern Caribbean Affairs*, Vol. 13, no. 4, 1987, Table 8, p. 21.

23. Ralph M. Henry, "A Reinterpretation of Labor Services of the Commonwealth Caribbean," in Anthony P. Maingot (ed.), *Small Country Development and International Labor Flows*, p. 120.

24. The World Bank, *Caribbean Region: Access, Quality and Efficiency in Education*, p. 12.

25. Ibid., p. 31.

26. Ibid., p. 39.

27. Recurrent Government Educational Expenditures in the six countries of the OECS examined in this study averaged 5.0 percent of Gross Domestic Product. The average for Barbados, Guyana, Jamaica, and Trinidad and Tobago was 4.7 percent. The average for East Africa was 4.2 percent, West Africa 4.2 percent, East Asia 3.5 percent, South Asia 1.6 percent, and Latin America 3.4 percent. See The World Bank, *Caribbean Region: Access, Quality, Efficiency in Education*, Tables 2.2 and 2.3, p. 25.

CHAPTER 9

A People
Without Borders

The contemporary migration from the West Indies is just the most recent episode in the region's history which militates against economic modernization. Slavery and post-Emancipation plantation agriculture did so too, as did British colonial policy. After independence, official economic policy did not seriously enough appreciate the requirements of modern technology. In several of the countries, Government policy allowed the public sector greatly to absorb resources, but without adequate demands being made on it to ensure that those resources were efficiently used. Elsewhere, tourism was allowed to become a leading sector of economic activity. But while tourism does raise income and earn foreign exchange, it is not the kind of industry which presses the society to enhance its technical capacity. And the region's educational system has been inadequate relative to its development needs.

But the migration has done something which those other elements of Caribbean history have not done, and therein lies hope for the future. For the migration has fundamentally reversed a salient element of regional history: the isolation of the people of the West Indies from the process of sustained and rapid technological change. Obviously the region has always been a participant in world product markets. But this was a narrow and limited participation and always using unsophisticated techniques. Particularly British colonial policy, in encouraging plantation agriculture, resulted in the Caribbean's becoming a backwater with respect to advanced production methods. Furthermore, nowhere in the region did the British encourage local businesses to gain access to the frontier of engineering and science. The same, unfortunately is true in the post-colonial period. Arnold McIntyre writes that in the present-day Caribbean, "neither at the regional nor national levels has careful consideration been given to the development of a pro-gramme for R&D activities or scientific and technological development."[1]

But the migration has a fundamentally different impact on the exposure of the West Indian people to modern technology. The massive and extended outflow from the Caribbean first to Great Britain and then later to the United States and Canada means the people of the region, for the first time, have lived in societies in which technological advances are rapid and continuous. In the diaspora they have become, in large numbers, a modern labor force, far different than the one which is resident in the Caribbean.

The numbers are indeed large. In 1990 the United States Census recorded 727,191 people living in that country who were born in the English-speaking Caribbean. In that same year 842,101 were listed as having a West Indies ancestry. This combined 1,569,292, when added to the roughly 225,000 West Indies people resident in Canada and 400,000 in Great Britain, means that about 2.2 million people with family roots in the English-speaking Carib-bean live outside of the region.[2] This statistic represents about 40 percent of the 5.3 million people resident in the West Indies countries included in this study. By any standard the emigration from the region has been enormous.

In 1980 the mean family income for West Indian families in the United States was estimated by Farley and Allen to be $(US) 20,990, a level which though lower than that achieved by comparable white families in that country is higher than similarly constituted African American, and Hispanic fami-lies.[3] To place this income figure in perspective, Graham Dann's survey of households in Barbados in the early 1980s indicates that over 80 percent of families there earned incomes of less than $(B) 11,280 per year.[4] Though using the prevailing exchange rate of $(B) 2 for $(US) 1 exaggerates the disparities in income levels between the two countries, these data suggest that West Indian households in coming to the United States have become effective participants in an entirely different economic environment than the one they left at home. If economic development has not come to the Carib-bean, then at least for a considerable percentage of West Indian people it can be said that they have gone to it.

An extensive discussion has raged over the years concerning the effects of this kind of brain drain. On one hand there is the argument that the region cannot hope to prosper when it loses its most ambitious and well educated people.[5] On the other hand, analysts such as Averille White believe that many of the emigres would not have found outlets for their talents if they had remained in the region. As a result White argues that "it is quite likely that the level of unemployment in the islands might be even higher were it not for this 'safety valve.'"[6]

Recently however, Ralph Henry has attempted to escape this dilemma in migration studies. Instead of considering the migration to be either a safety valve or a loss to the region, Henry has sought out means by which the West Indian people resident in the metropolitan country could be looked at as a resource, potentially available to the economies of the region. In this, he calls for a "redefinition of Commonwealth Caribbean space in the minds of the people and their governments." By stretching the definition of the boundary of the Caribbean societies to include the places in the United States, Canada and Great Britain, where there are concentrations of West Indian people, Henry hopes to take advantage of the "tremendous possibilities for entrepreneurial activities which would link Caribbean products with North American markets in a way that trade agreements ... have professed but failed to accomplish."[7] In another context he writes that "the time has come for the region to take steps to derive some benefit from this high level of emigration than merely remittance payments."[8]

Henry envisions two ways in which Caribbean people resident overseas might contribute to the economic development of their homelands. The first he describes as "redraining brains" and the second "outward higglering." Redraining brains refers to recruiting highly skilled Caribbean people to return to the region for relatively brief periods. Henry thinks that asking people to return permanently is asking them to give up too much and as a result such appeals have little prospect of success. Allowing overseas nationals to come to the region for brief periods of time, however, has two advantages. It might actually result in more overseas labor being made available in the West Indies than is the case at present and at the same time would allow highly skilled professionals to remain in touch with developments in their fields while still primarily residing in a metropolitan country. "Outward Higglering" refers to the possibility that linkages might be constructed between Caribbean-owned businesses abroad and at home. Networks constructed in this way, writes Henry, could "stimulate a flow of goods from the region initially with items that cater to 'ethnic markets' and probably extending beyond, to embrace new or non-traditional exports."[9] Thus it is that Henry is attempting to reverse the direction of benefits from education. Instead of people educated in the region using their skills in the North American labor force, he hopes that by attracting short-term workers and linking Caribbean and state-side businesses together, the West Indies will benefit from the accretion of skills that are accumulated by Caribbean people during their residence in the United States.

Henry's proposals to redefine labor services across geographic borders can be joined with more traditional proposals offered by David S. North and Judy A. Whitehead to enable the region better to use the resources present in the diaspora. These include the creation of a development bank located in the metropolitan country but dedicated to providing resources to the Caribbean, and the establishment of tax-exempt organizations to enable donors to receive tax benefits when they contribute funds to the West Indies. They also list actions which could be taken by the countries of the region and by the United States which would facilitate the flow of resources from North to South. Though not formally included in their list of recommendations, North and Whitehead also believe that absentee voting is desirable since it "would help bind emigres to the homeland."[10]

Both Henry and North and Whitehead are calling for an informal economic integration to be forged between the Caribbean people of the homeland and the diaspora. In this strategy the diaspora is viewed as part of a Greater Caribbean. The implicit hypothesis is that West Indians in the United States and Canada, and perhaps Great Britain, are present in sufficient numbers and in sufficient population concentrations to obtain a sense of themselves and engage in purposeful collective action. Ties of family and friends it is hoped can be institutionalized. The fact that the Caribbean people in North America are grouped geographically in a few metropolitan locations forms the basis of the belief that it might be possible successfully to appeal to their identity as West Indians to provide support for their compatriots who continue to reside in the region.

It must be said however that the dynamic implicit in a North–South integration of this kind may conflict with the kind of change necessary if the economic or political integration of the region itself is to be achieved. Trevor Farrell has argued that political integration of the Caribbean, possibly excluding Jamaica, is a sine quo non of regional economic development. His argument is that production and resource integration is required for the Caribbean to modernize. That in turn, he reasons, "raises the most fundamental questions of distribution and these can only be resolved politically."[11] But it is hard to see that both the kind of relationship between the people of the North and South that Henry envisions and the political unification of the region which is endorsed by Farrell can be achieved simultaneously. Precisely because resources — particularly human resources — are limited, it would appear to be more than enough for the region to attempt to accomplish just one of these goals, let alone both.

Both the question of which is more likely to be accomplished and which is more likely to yield decisive economic benefits must be addressed cautiously. There is very little empirical evidence upon which to base firm judgments. Tentatively, however, it would appear that the North–South integration is more likely to be accomplished, but that if regional political integration were to be achieved its long-term payoff would be bigger. The problem is that regional political integration has had such a vexed history, particularly centering on the failure of the West Indies Federation (1958–62) that most commentators have considered it beyond the possible. Even the West Indian Commission, a grouping of esteemed regional leaders with pronounced integrationist interests, was able only to bring itself to remark that "the goal of general West Indian unity at the political level remains for our people, it is clear, a sort of Holy Grail, shining on the edge of a distance too far away to matter for the time being."[12]

If this is so, the problem of economic modernization will ultimately reside in the hands of the individual Caribbean countries. It will be in the interest of each to try to tap into the good will and resources of the West Indian population in the United States, Canada and Great Britain. In this, a flow of skills, business acumen and financial resources should be encouraged in order to foster modern business enterprise in the region. For this to be successful, ultimately, however, the stock of human resources present in the nations of the Caribbean will have to be augmented. As we have seen, the migration greatly complicates that process, but this is a task which must be accomplished whether or not regional political integration is successful. There simply is no way that a country can be economically modern with a poorly educated labor force.

Just as tourism in the region has been organized on an individual country basis, and for the most part has grown and prospered, so it is possible that individual islands might be able to expand economically in the absence of integration. To be sure, there are efficiencies which will be lost in the absence of integration. Duplication of industries and redundant efforts to recruit industries could be avoided if it were possible to coordinate development efforts. But at the moment such cooperation looks as if it is not realistically on the West Indies agenda. As a result, it would appear to be a better choice to get on with the modernization effort on a country-by-country basis than to delay until some time in the indefinite future when regional cooperation will become a reality. The hope would be that with the passage of time, and in the context of positive economic modernization, the case for cooperation will become so compelling that it will be able to overcome the hostility to it associated with island parochialism. Something of the kind in fact has occurred with regional tourism, where a increased functional cooperation has become an important new development in advertising and product planning. Since this is so on an industry level, it might also become a reality on a more macro-economic plane. What is urgent at the moment, however, is that the people and policy makers of the region identify clearly what economic modernization requires and get on with the job of moving in the direction of those requisites.

There is an irony that to get to regional integration, it may be necessary to seek out a more informal integration with West Indians located outside of the geographic Caribbean. But the dynamic of the past has produced a situation in which these South to North linkages at the moment appear more likely to be forged than those among geographically proximate islands. If this is right, then the people of the region should get on with the job which is feasible at the moment and hope that nation-building will follow.

What this means is that the stock of human capital possessed by Caribbean people, no matter where they reside, should be viewed as a resource potentially available to the region. Modernization efforts in the West Indies, then, should include the constructing of institutions whereby those resources located in the diaspora become accessible to the nations of the Caribbean. In this way the people who are of, but not within, the narrowly defined boundaries of the geographic West Indies will be able to contribute to the modernization of their homeland.

NOTES

1. Arnold McIntyre, "Science and Technology Policy in Developing Countries: Some Implications for the Commonwealth Caribbean," *Bulletin of Eastern Caribbean Affairs*, Vol. 14, Nos. 5/6, November 1988 to February 1989, p. 16.

2. United States Bureau of the Census, *1990 Census of Population: Social and Economic Characteristics, 1990*, Cp-2-1, Table 26, p. 26 and Table 28, p. 28. Estimates of West Indies population in Great Britain and Canada come from Aaron Segal, *An Atlas of International Migration* (London: Hans Zell Publishers, 1993), p. 84.

3. Reynolds Farley and Walter R. Allen, *The Color Line and the Quality of Life in America* (New York: Russell Sage Foundation, 1987), Table 12.10, p. 404.

4. Graham Dann, *The Quality of Life in Barbados* (London: Macmillan Caribbean, 1984), Table 9, p. 33.

5. Bonham C. Richardson, "Caribbean Migrations 1838–1985," in Franklin W. Knight and Colin A. Palmer (eds.), *The Modern Caribbean* (Chapel Hill: The University of North Carolina Press, 1989), p. 224.

6. Averille White, "Eastern Caribbean Migrants in the USA: A Demographic Profile," p. 12.

7. Ralph M. Henry, "A Reinterpretation of Labor Services of the Commonwealth Caribbean," in Anthony P. Maingot (ed.), *Small Country Development and International Labor Flows: Experiences in the Caribbean*, pp. 130–131.

8. Ralph M. Henry, "Cooperation in Human Resource Utilisation in the Commonwealth Caribbean," *Bulletin of Eastern Caribbean Affairs*, Vol. 16, no. 1, March/April 1990, pp. 25–26.

9. Ibid., p. 26.

10. David S. North and Judy A. Whitehead, "Policy Recommendations for Improving the Utilization of Emigrant Resources in Eastern Caribbean Nations," in Anthony P. Maingot (ed.), *Small Country Development and International Labor Flows*, pp. 45–47.

11. M.A. Farrell, "The Caribbean State and Its Role in Economic Management," in Stanley Lalta and Marie Freckleton (eds.), *Caribbean Economic Development: The First Generation*, p. 209.

12. Report of the West indian Commission, *Time for Action* (Kingston, Jamaica: The Press–University of the West Indies, Second Edition, 1993), p. 24.

INDEX

For Product Safety Concerns and Information please contact our EU
representative GPSR@taylorandfrancis.com Taylor & Francis Verlag GmbH,
Kaufingerstraße 24, 80331 München, Germany

Printed and bound by CPI Group (UK) Ltd, Croydon, CR0 4YY
01/05/2025
01858345-0001